Perfectly Piec
Quilt Backs

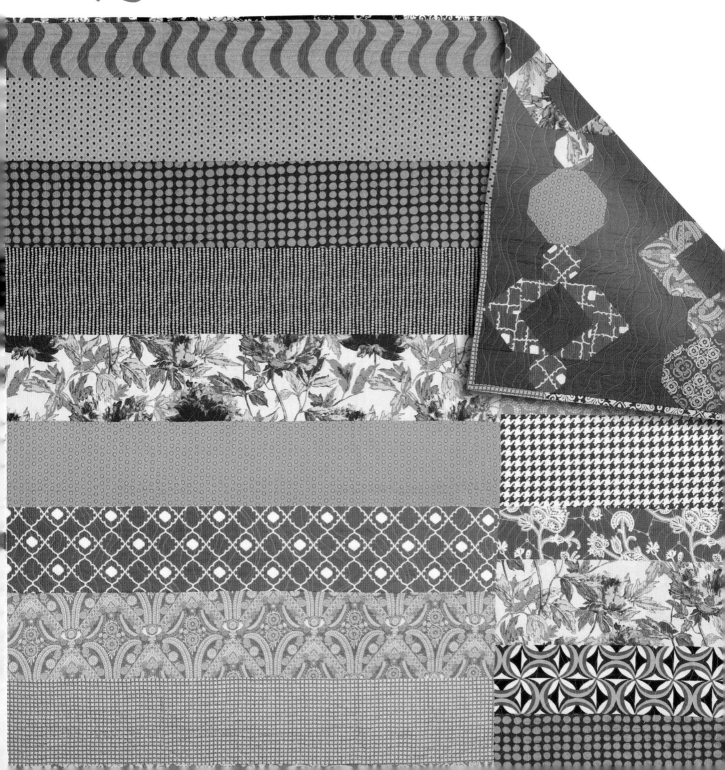

Perfectly Pieced Quilt Backs

Landauer Publishing, www.landauerpub.com, is an imprint of
Fox Chapel Publishing Company, Inc.

© 2023 by Kelly Young and Fox Chapel Publishing Company, Inc.,
903 Square Street, Mount Joy, PA 17552.

Project Team
Managing Editor: Gretchen Bacon
Acquisitions Editor: Amelia Johanson
Editor: Jeremy Hauck
Assistant Editor, Books: Christa Oestreich
Designer: Mary Ann Kahn
Photographer: Kelly Day Photography, Germantown, TN (www.kellydayportraits.com)
Illustrations: Kelly Young
Proofreader & Indexer: Jean Bissell

Sewing machine (11) © BERNINA of America, used with permission
Shutterstock used: AnnJane (128).

ISBN 978-1-63981-007-9

Library of Congress Control Number: 2023931776

We are always looking for talented authors. To submit an idea, please send a brief inquiry
to acquisitions@foxchapelpublishing.com.

Note to Professional Copy Services:
The publisher grants you permission to make up to six copies of any quilt patterns in this
book for any customer who purchased this book and states the copies are for personal use.

Printed in China
2 4 6 8 10 9 7 5 3 1

Perfectly Pieced Quilt Backs

The Scrap-Smart Guide to Finishing Quilts with Two-Sided Appeal

Kelly Young

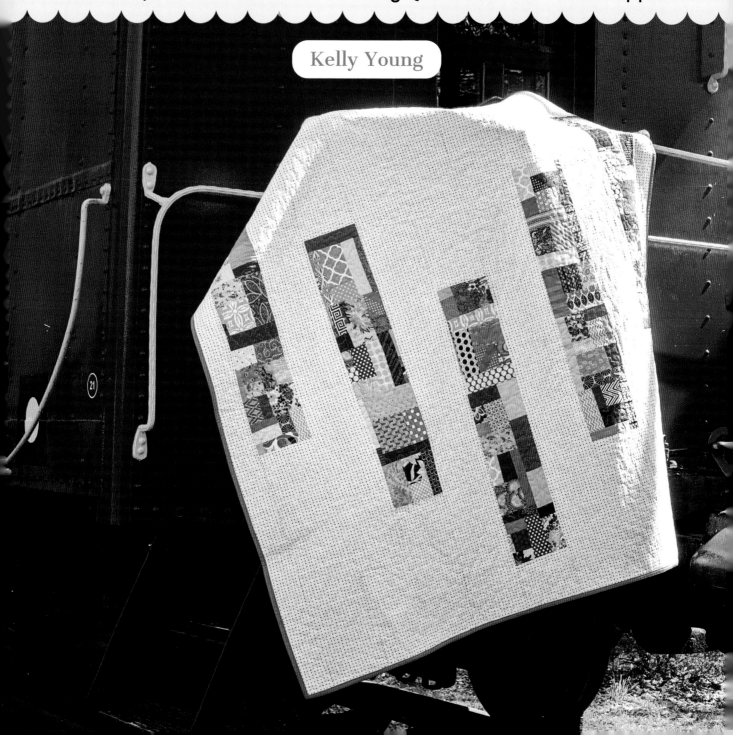

14

36

56

18

40

60

22

44

64

32

48

68

26

52

72

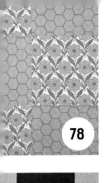

78

Contents

90

94

102

98

130

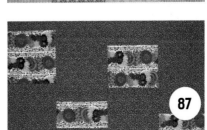

110

126

87

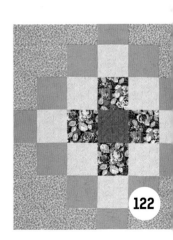

122

134

Introduction

The Case for a Pieced Quilt Back

Hooray! You've just spent hours on a beautiful quilt top, and it's finally all done. Now you're ready to think about turning that lovely top into a finished quilt. At this point, it can be tempting to skip right to thoughts about the quilting designs that will give it texture and really bring it to life. But not so fast! You're missing out on an opportunity to make your quilt truly unique—the backing!

I know, you're ready to get your quilt finished, and you don't want anything too complicated. You don't want to have to figure out fabric requirements for piecing your backing. And you definitely don't want to spend too much time on this step. Great! We're in agreement.

With this book, I'll show you that a fast, fun, and easy quilt backing is doable, I'll give you all of the fabric requirements and instructions you'll need for several quilt sizes, and you'll have all the guidance you need to make every part of your quilt special. Your quilt is worth it, but if you need a few more reasons . . .

The Double Bar quilt back (page 7) uses scraps of various sizes.

1. **It adds something extra.** Though I currently live in Tennessee, I was born and raised in Louisiana, and back home, we have a French word, *lagniappe* (pronounced "lan-yap"), that means "a little something extra." Think of a pieced quilt backing as a little lagniappe for the recipient. What a wonderful surprise!

2. **Use that fabric stash.** Many of these pieced quilt backings are made from leftovers from the front of the quilt, and it feels like a win to use them up, rather than adding them to the scrap bin. Others are made from stash and yardage, and it's fun and easy to sew those big pieces together for a quick finish.

3. **Use a variety of fabric!** I love tons of print variety in my quilts, and sometimes that means that I make quilts with more fabrics than required by the pattern. That's okay though, because that means there are lots of leftovers for the back!

4. **Guilt-free fabric shopping.** By using up your fabrics on the front AND the back of your quilt, the next time you want to add more to your stash, you can do so guilt free!

5. **There's no need to search for a single backing fabric.** When your backing has scraps from the front of your quilt, or several coordinating fabrics, you won't need to worry that you can't find one single fabric to bring it all together. Your backing will always coordinate perfectly!

6. **It doesn't take a lot of time—really!** I'm not talking about making double-sided quilts here. These backings are simple, but will complement your quilt top beautifully. After all of the time you spent on it, isn't your quilt worth a few extra minutes?

PART 1

Quilt Back Basics . . . . . .

Before we jump right into the cache of quilt back patterns, there are a few important points to keep in mind.

SIMPLICITY

Where quilt backs are concerned, simplicity is the name of the game. Nobody wants to spend days on a complicated quilt back. Though some of the designs in this book are simpler than others, none of them are terribly time consuming. Many of these quilt backs can be completed in an hour or two, and none should take longer than an afternoon. Luckily, your quilt back doesn't need to be labor intensive to be unique!

For beginners, these designs could even be a great starting point. Simply use the the backs as your quilt front, and you'll be mastering the basics in no time!

SIZING

Each quilt back pattern in the book contains full fabric requirements, as well as cutting and piecing instructions for Lap, Twin XL, and Queen sizes. That being said, as quilters we all know that a quilt can be made in any size we like. So, you'll see some variation in the backing sizes based on the design and the fabric cuts used in the pattern.

If you're not sure about what size to make your quilt, the chart on the right is a helpful guide showing finished quilt measurements.

Because quilts can have such a wide variety of sizes, it stands to reason that quilt backs be different sizes too! If your quilt is a size that doesn't quite fit the backing pattern as listed, that's okay! It's easy to modify the size by adding an extra strip to one side to make it larger, or you can even make it a little smaller if you need to. Just remember:

- **Quilt backs are made to be cut.** The finished size of the quilt will be determined by the front, not the back. Keep that in mind when you're looking at the back of a finished quilt. The backing always starts out bigger, and the patterns in this book give the backing size before basting and trimming to fit your quilt top.

- **Make it larger!** Your backing should be at least four inches larger than your quilt top (in both width and length). This gives you two inches of wiggle room all around the quilt while basting.

- **Sizing rules are different for longarm quilting.** If you're taking your quilt to a longarm quilter, your backing should be even bigger. Most longarm quilters like the backing to be about ten inches larger than the quilt top (in both width and length), giving them five inches all around the quilt. This extra fabric is used to load the quilt onto the rollers of the quilt frame. This fabric will still be trimmed away after quilting.

Quilt Size	Width	Length
Crib	36"–45" (91.4–114.3cm)	45"–58" (114.3–147.3cm)
Lap	54"–60" (137.2–152.4cm)	60"–74" (152.4–188cm)
Twin XL	56"–70" (142.2–177.8cm)	84"–108" (213.4–274.3cm)
Queen	78"–84" (198.1–213.4cm)	95"–108" (241.3–274.3cm)
King	90"–100" (228.6–254cm)	95"–108" (241.3–274.3cm)

Use a Focus Stripe back (page 98) to highlight a favorite fabric.

TOOLS AND OTHER HELPFUL HINTS

The tools needed for making a pieced quilt back are the same as the ones needed for quilting.

PERFECT PIECING

The quilt back patterns in this book are all constructed with simple, basic piecing techniques. There are just a couple of things to keep in mind:

- **Seam allowance.** Always use ¼" (0.5cm) seam allowance and sew the pieces right-sides together. A ¼" (0.5cm) seam allowance is standard for quilting, and is also used for making a pieced quilt back.

- **Pressing.** Press the seams of your quilt back toward the darker fabric, OR press seams open. Try not to vigorously rub the iron back and forth over your quilt back. This can distort your fabric, resulting in a backing with ripples. You'll want a crisp, smooth backing when it's time to baste.

Think Through Your Scraps

With so many different ways to use your leftovers on the back of your quilt, before selecting a pattern, first take a look at your scraps to help you choose one that will maximize what you have on hand. Are your scraps regular or irregular in size? Are they large or small? How many scraps do you have? Answering these questions before choosing a backing design will help you match your pattern choice to your unique quilt scraps. The designs shown in the Scrap and Leftover Backs section are grouped by scrap size to help make this process easy.

Gear Up

1. **Sewing machine.** Essential for any quilting project, a sewing machine can easily create straight and curved lines. It also makes repetitive tasks a breeze. Use the included manual to familiarize yourself with all the features on your sewing machine. You'll need a ¼" (0.5cm) foot, walking foot, and free-motion quilting foot. Learn more about Walking Foot and Free-Motion Quilting on page 142.

2. **Rotary cutter.** A nice, sharp blade makes cutting yardage a breeze.

3. **Cutting mat.** Unlike a table or board, this absorbs the impact of a blade. Perfect companion for a rotary cutter when squaring off blocks. The larger the better!

4. **Acrylic ruler.** A long, 24" (61cm) ruler is helpful for cutting larger pieces of yardage. Use as a straight edge when cutting as well as a measuring tool.

5. **Straight pins.** These are optional, but can be helpful for holding fabric pieces in place while sewing them together.

6. **Scissors.** You'll need sharp scissors for trimming your pieces and cutting large pieces of fabric. Make sure you are using fabric scissors so it evenly glides over the material.

7. **Cotton thread.** My favorite is Aurifil 50 wt., but as long as you choose high-quality cotton thread, any brand will work.

8. **Seam ripper.** Mistakes happen sometimes, and when they do, your seam ripper is your friend.

9. **Iron and ironing board.** Use your iron's hottest setting to press your quilt pieces or quilt back to make it nice and smooth. Pressing your seam allowances is essential to keeping your quilt back flat and wrinkle-free.

10. **Starch or starch alternative.** I prefer this over steam. It adds a little crispness to the fabric, making it easier to handle and helps the seams lay flat. Follow package directions, and test on a piece of scrap fabric before using on your intended fabric.

11. **Safety pins.** These are essential for basting. I like the larger ones.

12. **Painter's or masking tape.** Another essential tool for basting, and for keeping the backing and quilt top lined up properly. It can also be used for the corner-to-corner sewing technique in some quilt patterns.

13. **Marking pencil.** This is an optional tool for the corner-to-corner sewing technique in some quilt patterns.

Sewing machine

Photo courtesy of BERNINA of America

Masking tape

Acrylic ruler

Rotary cutter

Cotton thread

Straight pins

Starch

Seam ripper

Marking pencil

Scissors

Safety pins

Cutting mat

PART 2

Scrap and Leftover Backs

Your quilt top is all finished and you're looking at a pile of leftovers on your cutting table. Wouldn't it be wonderful to use them right away, rather than adding them to your scrap bins? Rest assured! There's a pattern that will help you turn those leftovers into a unique quilt back that will use up every precious piece.

• • •

Large leftover scraps really shine in a Chunky quilt back (page 56).

Coin Strip

SKILL LEVEL ✳ ✳ ✳ ✳ ✳
Confident Beginner

A fabric coin is a fun term used to describe a small rectangle of fabric that is relatively short but narrow. When they're sewn together, they look like a stack of coins. The coin strip backing is great for those quilt patterns that only leave behind smaller pieces. The fun little strip on the back is the perfect finishing touch.

FINISHED BACKING DIMENSIONS

Lap 68" x 72" (172.7 x 182.9cm)

Twin XL 77" x 108" (195.6 x 274.3cm)

Queen 90" x 108" (228.6 x 274.3cm)

Materials Yardage is based on 42" (106.7cm) wide fabric.

	Lap	Twin XL	Queen
Fabric Coins	Leftover pieces of fabric measuring 6"–8" (15.2–20.3cm) in length	Leftover pieces of fabric measuring 8"–10" (20.3–25.4 cm) in length	
Background fabric	3⅔ yards (3.4m)	5¼ yards (4.8m)	5⅔ yards (5.2m)

Cutting All measurements include ¼" (0.5cm) seam allowances.

	Lap	Twin XL	Queen
Fabric Coins, cut	Cut each coin to the same length, as determined by your scraps, 6"–8" (15.2–20.3cm) long. Coins may be different widths or a single, consistent width.	Cut each coin to the same length, as determined by your scraps, 8"–10" (20.3–25.4cm) long. Coins may be different widths or a single, consistent width.	
From the background fabric, cut	3 strips, 20" x 42" (50.8 x 106.7cm) leave the remaining length uncut, 72" x 42" (182.9 x 106.7cm)	3 strips, 27" x 42" (68.6 x 106.7cm) leave the remaining length uncut, 108" x 42" (274.3 x 106.7cm)	3 strips, 32" x 42" (81.3 x 106.7cm) leave the remaining length uncut, 108" x 42" (274.3 x 106.7cm)

Note: Seam allowances should be pressed after each join. Press open or press alternating rows/columns toward the darker fabric based on your preference.

For the corresponding quilt top, Folk Dance, see page 146.

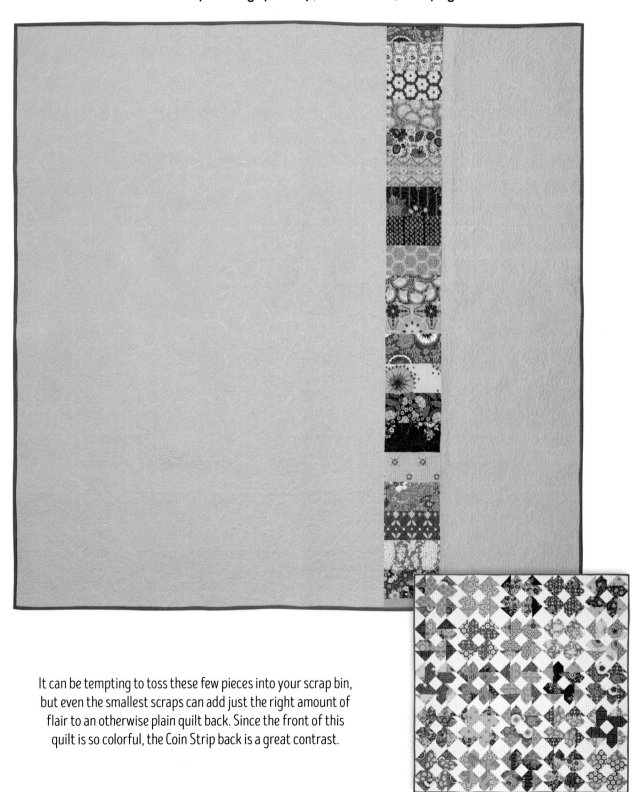

It can be tempting to toss these few pieces into your scrap bin, but even the smallest scraps can add just the right amount of flair to an otherwise plain quilt back. Since the front of this quilt is so colorful, the Coin Strip back is a great contrast.

MAKE THE COIN STRIP

1. For the Lap size, lay out the coins and sew them into one long strip measuring 6"–8" (15.2–20.3cm) wide and at least 72" (182.9cm) long.

2. For the Twin XL size, lay out the coins and sew them into one long strip measuring 8"–10" (20.3–25.4cm) wide and at least 108" (274.3cm) long.

3. For the Queen size, lay out the coins and sew them into two long strips measuring 8"–10" (20.3–25.4cm) wide and at least 108" (274.3cm) long. Sew the two coin strips together to make a double coin strip, 16"–20" (40.6 x 50.8cm) wide and at least 108" (274.3cm) long.

ASSEMBLE THE QUILT BACK

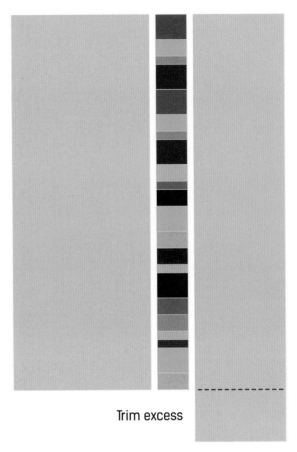

Trim excess

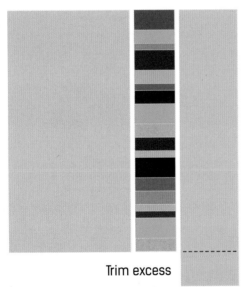

Trim excess

1. For the Lap size, sew the three 20" x 42" (50.8 x 106.7cm) background fabric strips together, end to end, to make one long strip 20" (50.8cm) wide. Then, refer to the Quilt Assembly Diagram to lay out the uncut length of background fabric, coin strip, and 20" (50.8cm) wide strip of background fabric into three columns as shown. Sew the columns together and trim the excess length from the 20" (50.8cm) wide background strip to complete the quilt back.

2. For the Twin XL size, sew the three 27" x 42" (68.6 x 106.7cm) background fabric strips together, end to end, to make one long strip 27" (68.6cm) wide. Then, refer to the Quilt Assembly Diagram to lay out the uncut length of background fabric, coin strip, and 27" (68.6cm) wide strip of background fabric into three columns as shown. Sew the columns together and trim the excess length from the 27" (68.6cm) wide background strip to complete the quilt back.

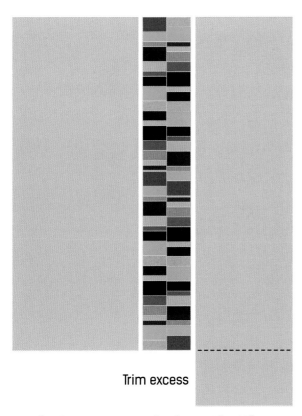

Trim excess

3. For the Queen size, sew the three 32" x 42" (81.3 x 106.7cm) background fabric strips together, end to end, to make one long strip 32" (81.3cm) wide. Then, refer to the Quilt Assembly Diagram to lay out the uncut length of background fabric, double coin strip, and 32" (81.3cm) wide strip of background fabric into three columns as shown. Sew the columns together and trim the excess length from the 32" (81.3cm) wide background strip to complete the quilt back.

If you don't have quite enough coins to cover the entire length of the quilt back, you can fill in with extra background fabric. It will still look great!

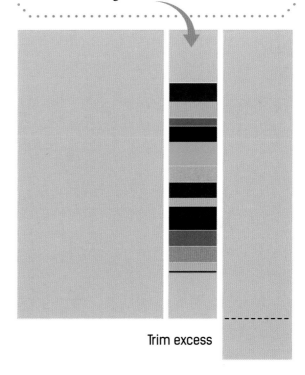

Trim excess

FINISH THE QUILT

Refer to the Basting and Quilt Finishing section on page 138 for instructions on basting, quilting, and binding your quilt.

4. Layer the backing, batting, and quilt top and baste the layers together. Hand- or machine-quilt as desired.

Framed Orphan

SKILL LEVEL ✻ ✻ ✻ ✻ ✻
Confident Beginner

Have an extra block from your quilt pattern or even from a Block of the Month project? Don't let it go to waste. This backing is the perfect place to show it off! With a couple of coordinating prints, this design couldn't be easier!

FINISHED BACKING DIMENSIONS

Lap 72" x 78" (182.9 x 198.1cm)

Twin XL 72" x 102" (182.9 x 259.1cm)

Queen 90" x 102" (228.6 x 259.1cm)

Materials Yardage is based on 42" (106.7cm) wide fabric.

One orphan quilt block measuring 18½" (47cm) or smaller.

If your orphan block is smaller than 18½" (47cm) square, sew a border to each side to increase the size of the block to 18½" (47cm) square. The orphan block shown measures 12½" (31.8cm) square, with a 3½" (8.9cm) border sewn to each side of the block.

	Lap	Twin XL	Queen
Print A (dark green)	2⅓ yards (2.1m)	3⅛ yards (2.9m)	4⅛ yards (3.8m)
Print B (red)	2⅞ yards (2.6m)	2⅛ yards (1.9m)	2⅛ yards (1.9m)
Print C (cream)*	¼ yard (22.9cm)	¼ yard (22.9cm)	¼ yard (22.9cm)

*Only if needed to widen the orphan block unit to 18½" (47cm) square

Cutting All measurements include ¼" (0.5cm) seam allowances.

	Lap	Twin XL	Queen
From print A (dark green), cut	1 strip, 27½" x 42" (69.9 x 106.7cm), subcut 2 rectangles, 18½" x 27½" (47 x 69.9cm) 2 strips, 27½" x 42" (69.9 x 106.7cm)	4 strips, 27½" x 42" (69.9 x 106.7cm)	4 strips, 36½" x 42" (92.7 x 106.7cm)
From print B (red), cut	1 strip, 27½" x 42" (69.9 x 106.7cm), subcut 2 rectangles, 18½" x 27½" (47 x 69.9cm) 1 strip, 18½" x 42" (47 x 106.7cm) 1 strip, 18½" x 42" (47 x 106.7cm), subcut 1 square, 18½" (47cm)	4 strips, 18½" x 42" (47 x 106.7cm)	4 strips, 18½" x 42" (47 x 106.7cm), subcut 4 strips, 18½" x 36½" (47 x 92.7cm)
From print C (cream), cut if needed	Cut rectangles of equal width and attach to each side of the orphan block to widen it. Trim the orphan block unit to 18½" (47cm) square.		

Note: Seam allowances should be pressed after each join. Press open or press alternating rows/columns toward the darker fabric based on your preference.

While this particular quilt back has a holiday theme, selecting colors and prints to complement
your own orphan block will ensure your backing is just right for your quilt!

ASSEMBLE THE QUILT BACK

1. Refer to the Lap Quilt Assembly Diagram to lay out the orphan block unit, print A rectangles, and print B rectangles as shown. Join the three units in each row. Press the seams in row 1 and 3 away from center, and row 2 toward the center. Join the three rows together to complete the quilt back.

2. For the Twin XL size, refer to the Twin XL Quilt Assembly Diagram to lay out the orphan block unit, print A rectangles, and print B rectangles as shown. Join the three units in each row. Press the seams in row 1 and 3 away from center, and row 2 toward the center. Join the three rows together to complete the quilt back.

FINISH THE QUILT

Refer to the Basting and Quilt Finishing section on page 138 for instructions on basting, quilting, and binding your quilt.

4. Layer the backing, batting, and quilt top and baste the layers together. Hand- or machine-quilt as desired.

3. For the Queen size, refer to the Queen Quilt Assembly Diagram to lay out the orphan block unit, print A rectangles, and print B rectangles as shown. Join the three units in each row. Press the seams in row 1 and 3 away from center, and row 2 toward the center. Join the three rows together to complete the quilt back.

If you're working on a themed quilt, this block is a great way to bring a little of the look onto the back. Imagine a sailboat floating in a sea of blues, or a fresh flower among a garden of greens. The possibilities are endless!

Cross Purposes

SKILL LEVEL ✳ ✳ ✳ ✳ ✳
Confident Beginner

If you have only a few narrow scrap pieces left over from your quilt, you might think you're out of luck for a pieced quilt back. Thankfully, the Cross Purposes pattern will put them to good use. These scattered cross blocks are so easy to put together, but they make a fun impact on this backing.

FINISHED BACKING DIMENSIONS

Lap 66" x 72" (167.6 x 182.9cm)

Twin XL 80" x 108" (203.2 x 274.3cm)

Queen 96" x 108" (243.8 x 274.3cm)

Materials Yardage is based on 42" (106.7cm) wide fabric.

	Lap	Twin XL	Queen
Scrap rectangles	Narrow scrap rectangles, 2"–4" (5.1–10.2cm) wide and at least 12½" (31.8cm) long. Two rectangles each from five fabrics	Narrow scrap rectangles, 2"–4" (5.1–10.2cm) wide and at least 12½" (31.8cm) long. Two rectangles each from eight fabrics	
Non-directional Background fabric	3⅞ yards (3.5m)	6⅞ yards (6.3m)	7½ yards (6.9m)

Cutting All measurements include ¼" (0.5cm) seam allowances.

	Lap	Twin XL	Queen
Scrap rectangles, cut	Straighten the edges of each narrow scrap rectangle, and trim to 12½" (31.8cm) long.		
From the background fabric, cut	2 strips, 12" x 42" (30.5 x 106.7cm), subcut 5 squares, 12" (30.5cm) 5 strips, 12½" x 42" (31.8 x 106.7cm) 2 strips, 12½" x 42" (31.8 x 106.7cm), subcut 5 squares, 12½" (31.8cm) 4 strips, 6½" x 42" (16.5 x 106.7cm)	3 strips, 12" x 42" (30.5 x 106.7cm), subcut 8 squares,12" (30.5cm) 8 strips, 12½" x 42" (31.8 x 106.7cm) 3 strips, 27" x 42" (68.6 x 106.7cm), subcut 8 rectangles, 12½" x 27" (31.8 x 68.6cm) 4 strips, 6½" x 42" (16.5 x 106.7cm)	3 strips, 12" x 42" (30.5 x 106.7cm), subcut 8 squares, 12" (30.5cm) 16 strips, 12½" x 42", (31.8 x 106.7cm) 5 strips, 6½" x 42", (16.5 x 106.7cm), from one strip, subcut 2 rectangles 6½" x 21" (16.5 x 53.3cm)

Note: Seam allowances should be pressed after each join. Press open or press alternating rows/columns toward the darker fabric based on your preference.

These simple cross shapes are reminiscent of twinkling stars or plus signs, and the scattered layout gives this back some whimsy.

MAKE THE CROSS BLOCKS

1. Cut a 12" (30.5cm) background square in half vertically, and sew a scrap rectangle between the two halves. Press and trim any excess length from the scrap strip.

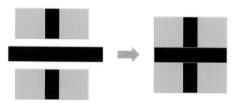

2. Then cut the block in half *in the opposite direction* and sew the second scrap strip between the two halves. Press and trim the finished block to 12½" (31.8cm) square. Make five total blocks for the Lap size, or eight total blocks for the Twin XL and Queen sizes.

ASSEMBLE THE QUILT BACK

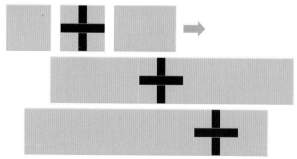

3. For the Lap size, sew a 12½" (31.8cm) background square and a 12½" x 42" (31.8 x 106.7cm) background strip together, end to end, to make one long strip, 12½" x 54" (31.8 x 137.1cm). Then sew this long strip to *both ends* of a cross block to create a loop. Cut the background strip crosswise in a random place to make a row that measures 12½" x 66" (31.8 x 167.6cm). Make five rows, cutting each loop in a different place to make the cross blocks randomly scattered across the quilt back.

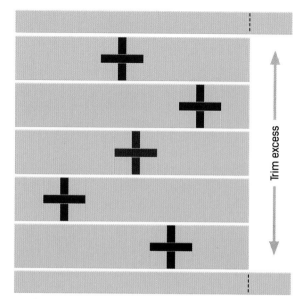

Trim excess

4. Refer to the Lap Quilt Assembly Diagram to lay out the rows and sew them together. Then sew two 6½" x 42" (16.5 x 106.7cm) background strips together, end to end, to make one long strip, 6½" x 84" (16.5 x 213.4cm). Sew the long strip to the top of the rows and trim away the excess length. Repeat this process on the bottom of the rows to complete the quilt back.

5. For the Twin XL size, sew a 12½" x 27" (31.8 x 68.6cm) background rectangle and a 12½" x 42" (31.8 x 106.7cm) background strip together, end to end, to make one long strip, 12½" x 69" (31.8 x 175.3cm). Then sew this long strip to *both ends* of a cross block to create a loop. Cut the background strip crosswise in a random place to make a row that measures 12½" x 80" (31.8 x 203.2cm). Make eight rows, cutting each loop in a different place to make the cross blocks randomly scattered across the quilt back.

Work from top to bottom. Cut the loop for the top row and lay it out before making the next cut. Continue cutting and laying out each loop to ensure the blocks are scattered the way you like them.

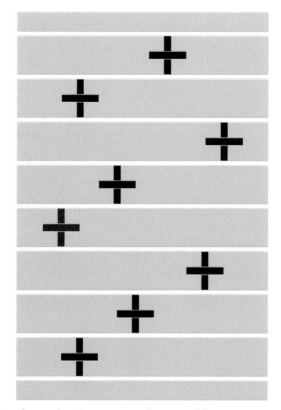

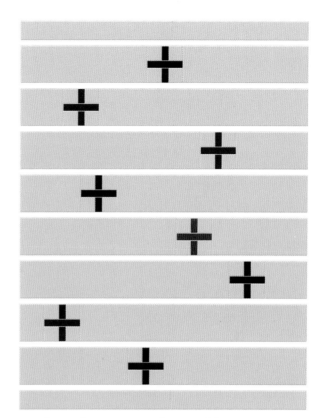

6. Refer to the Twin XL Quilt Assembly Diagram to lay out the rows and sew them together. Sew two 6½" x 42" (16.5 x 106.7cm) background strips together, end to end, to make one long strip, 6½" x 84" (16.5 x 213.4cm). Sew the long strip to the top of the rows and trim away the excess length. Repeat this process on the bottom of the rows to complete the quilt back.

7. For the Queen size, sew two 12½" x 42" (31.8 x 106.7cm) background strips together, end to end, to make one long strip, 12½" x 84" (31.8 x 213.4cm). Then sew this long strip to *both ends* of a cross block to create a loop. Cut the background strip crosswise in a random place to make a row that measures 12½" x 96" (31.8 x 243.8cm). Make eight rows, cutting each loop in a different place to make the cross blocks randomly scattered across the quilt back.

8. Refer to the Queen Quilt Assembly Diagram to lay out the rows and sew them together. Sew two 6½" x 42" (16.5 x 106.7cm) background strips and one 6½" x 21" (16.5 x 53.3cm) background rectangle together, end to end, to make one long strip, 6½" x 105" (16.5 x 266.7cm). Sew the long strip to the top of the rows and trim away the excess length. Repeat this process on the bottom of the rows to complete the quilt back.

FINISH THE QUILT

Refer to the Basting and Quilt Finishing section on page 138 for instructions on basting, quilting, and binding your quilt.

9. Layer the backing, batting, and quilt top and baste the layers together. Hand- or machine-quilt as desired.

Tallies

Tallies is another fun backing for using up all of your leftover bits and pieces. No scrap is too small! Long, narrow improv strips are arranged in a simple but easy design that will make your scraps truly shine.

FINISHED BACKING DIMENSIONS

Lap 66" x 72" (167.6 x 182.9cm)

Twin XL 84" x 108" (213.4 x 274.3cm)

Queen 94" x 108" (238.8 x 274.3cm)

Materials
Yardage is based on 42" (106.7cm) wide fabric.

	Lap	Twin XL	Queen
Main fabric	3 yards (2.7m)	6¼ yards (5.7m)	7 yards (6.4m)
Smaller scraps-squares, rectangles, and strips	Enough scraps to make 5 blocks, 6½" x 30½" (16.5 x 77.5cm)		

Cutting
All measurements include ¼" (0.5cm) seam allowances.

	Lap	Twin XL	Queen
From the main fabric, cut	11 strips, 6½" x 42" (16.5 x 106.7cm) 1 strip, 30½" x 42" (77.5 x 106.7cm), subcut 6 rectangles, 6½" x 30½" (16.5 x 77.5cm)	9 strips, 6½" x 42" (16.5 x 106.7cm) 1 strip, 30½" x 42" (77.5 x 106.7cm), subcut 4 rectangles, 6½" x 30½" (16.5 x 77.5cm) 2 strips, 15½" x 42" (39.4 x 106.7cm) 1 strip, 30½" x 42" (77.5 x 106.7cm), subcut 2 rectangles, 15½" x 30½" (39.4 x 77.5cm) 4 strips, 18" x 42" (45.7 x 106.7cm)	9 strips, 6½" x 42" (16.5 x 106.7cm) 1 strip, 30½" x 42" (77.5 x 106.7cm), subcut 4 rectangles, 6½" x 30½" (16.5 x 77.5cm) 2 strips, 20½" x 42" (52.1 x 106.7cm) 1 strip, 30½" x 42" (77.5 x 106.7cm), subcut 2 rectangles, 20½" x 30½" (52.1 x 77.5cm) 5 strips, 18" x 42" (45.7 x 106.7cm) from one strip, subcut 2 rectangles, 10½" x 18" (26.7 x 45.7cm)

Note: Seam allowances should be pressed after each join. Press open or press alternating rows/columns toward the darker fabric based on your preference.

Improv quilting breaks free of the rigid lines that define other quilt blocks. My improv blocks are made with mostly square or rectangular pieces, but if you want to piece your improv blocks with different shapes and angles, go for it! That's part of the fun! As long as your improv blocks end up the correct size, you can't go wrong.

MAKE THE IMPROV BLOCKS

1. Start by sorting your scrap pieces into four piles according to size.

- **Bits (smallest scraps):** squares or rectangles roughly the size of your hand, without fingers

- **Pieces (a little larger):** squares or rectangles roughly the size of your entire hand, including fingers

- **Strings (shorter narrow scraps):** skinny scraps that are about 12" (30.5cm) or shorter

- **Strips (longer narrow scraps):** skinny scraps that are longer than 12" (30.5cm), up to the entire width-of-fabric

3. Choose a scrap from the pile of "pieces" that is the same length or slightly longer than the pair of sewn bits, and sew the piece to the side of the unit. Trim away any excess length. Repeat this process for all remaining pairs of sewn bits.

2. Choose two scraps from the pile of "bits" that are similar in length, and sew them together. Trim away any excess length. Repeat this process three times to make four pairs of sewn bits.

4. Next, add a scrap from the strings pile to the sewn unit. Repeat this process for the remaining sewn units. At this point, each sewn unit should have four different scraps.

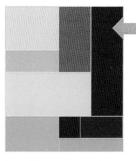

5. Sew two of the units together. Turn the units, or add additional scraps if necessary to make them fit together. Then, repeat this process for the second pair of sewn units.

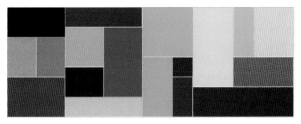

6. Sew the two units from step 5 together to make one longer improv unit. Turn the units, or add additional scraps if necessary to make them fit together. Continue adding scraps to the improv unit until it is the desired size for the quilt back. Trim the improv blocks to size if necessary. Make five improv blocks, 6½" x 30½" (16.5 x 77.5cm).

Put away that rotary cutter! While building the improv blocks, sharp scissors are a fast, easy way to trim away the excess length from your scraps. Save the rotary cutter for squaring up your improv blocks and trimming them to size.

ASSEMBLE THE QUILT BACK

7. *For all sizes,* subcut one 6½" x 10½" (16.5 x 26.7cm) rectangle from a 6½" x 42" (16.5 x 106.7cm) background strip, and sew the improv block between the two pieces as shown to make one improv column. Repeat this process to make three identical improv columns.

8. Then, subcut one 6½" x 42" (16.5 x 106.7cm) rectangle into two equal rectangles, each 6½" x 21" (16.5 x 53.3cm), and sew an improv block between the two pieces as shown. Repeat this process to make the remaining improv column.

9. Sew one 6½" x 42" (16.5 x 106.7cm) strip and one 6½" x 30½" (16.5 x 77.5cm) rectangle together to make one sashing strip. Repeat this process to make four total sashing strips.

When building the improv units, sew the scraps randomly, with some vertical seams and some horizontal seams. This gives the improv block its unique look.

10. Lay out the five improv columns and four sashing strips and sew them together as shown to complete the improv section of the backing.

It isn't necessary to always use a solid background fabric with your improv blocks. My Tallies quilt back uses a fabric with small black and white plusses, and it still allows plenty of contrast.

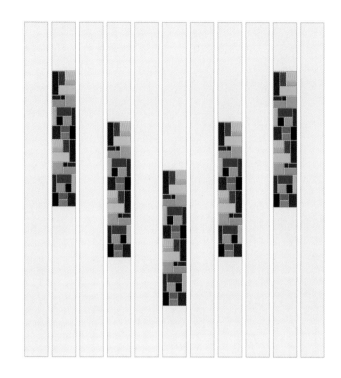

11. For the Lap size, refer to the Lap Quilt Assembly Diagram and sew one 6½" x 42" (16.5 x 106.7cm) strip and one 6½" x 30½" (16.5 x 77.5cm) rectangle together to make one long strip, 6½" x 72" (16.5 x 182.9cm), and sew it to the side of the improv section. Repeat this process on the other side to complete the quilt back.

12a. For the Twin XL size, refer to the Twin Quilt Assembly Diagram and sew one 15½" x 42" (39.4 x 106.7cm) strip and one 15½" x 30½" (39.4 x 77.5cm) rectangle together to make one long strip, 15½" x 72" (39.4 x 182.9cm), and sew it to the side of the improv section. Repeat this process on the other side.

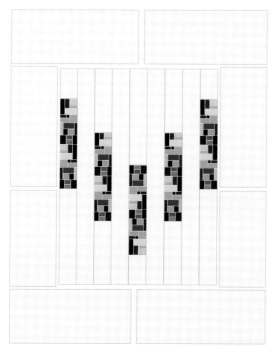

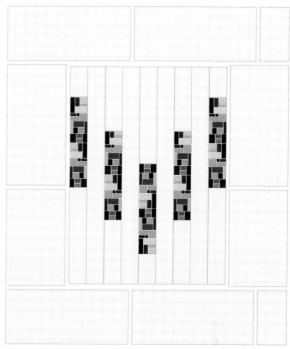

12b. Then, sew two 18" x 42" (45.7 x 106.7cm) strips together to make one long strip, 18" x 84" (45.7 x 213.4cm) and sew it to the top of the improv section. Repeat this process, and sew the strip to the bottom of the improv section to complete the quilt back.

13a. For the Queen size, refer to the Queen Quilt Assembly Diagram and sew one 20½" x 42" (52.1 x 106.7cm) strip and one 20½" x 30½" (52.1 x 77.5cm) rectangle together to make one long strip, 20½" x 72" (52.1 x 182.9cm), and sew it to the side of the improv section. Repeat this process on the other side.

13b. Then, sew two 18" x 42" (45.7 x 106.7cm) strips and one 10½" x 18" (26.7 x 45.7cm) rectangle together to make one long strip, 18" x 94" (45.7 x 238.8cm) and sew it to the top of the improv section. Repeat this process, and sew the strip to the bottom of the improv section to complete the quilt back.

FINISH THE QUILT

Refer to the Basting and Quilt Finishing section on page 138 for instructions on basting, quilting, and binding your quilt.

14. Layer the backing, batting, and quilt top and baste the layers together. Hand- or machine-quilt as desired.

Every Little Bit

SKILL LEVEL ✳ ✳ ✳ ✳ ✳
Beginner

If you need a backing to utilize lots of smaller scraps, look no further! Sewing those little scraps into larger chunks of improv-pieced, "created fabric" is super easy, and nothing goes to waste!

FINISHED BACKING DIMENSIONS

Lap 72" x 72" (182.9 x 182.9cm)

Twin XL 84" x 108" (213.4 x 274.3cm)

Queen 99" x 108" (251.5 x 274.3cm)

Materials Yardage is based on 42" (106.7cm) wide fabric.

	Lap	Twin XL	Queen
Main fabric	3 yards (2.7m)	5 yards (4.6m)	6 yards (5.5m)
Smaller scraps– squares, rectangles, and strips	Enough scraps to make 6 blocks, 12½" x 12½" (31.8 x 31.8cm)	Enough scraps to make 6 blocks, 18½" x 18½" (47 x 47cm)	Enough scraps to make 6 blocks, 15½" x 18½" (39.4 x 47cm)

Cutting All measurements include ¼" (0.5cm) seam allowances.

	Lap	Twin XL	Queen
From the main fabric, cut	2 strips, 18" x 42" (45.7 x 106.7cm) *The remaining piece of fabric should measure 2 yards, 72" x 42" (182.9 x 106.7cm) after the selvages are removed	3 strips, 24" x 42" (61 x 106.7cm) *The remaining piece of fabric should measure 3 yards, 108" x 42" (274.3 x 106.7cm) after the selvages are removed	Cut the backing into two equal lengths, each 42" x 108" (106.7 x 274.3cm)

Note: Seam allowances should be pressed after each join. Press open or press alternating rows/columns toward the darker fabric based on your preference.

For the corresponding quilt top, Waverunner, see page 146.

The wavy line quilting design complements the blue and aqua prints on this quilt, giving the impression of waves at sea. The darker fabric choice on the back allows the quilting to really shine and reveals the meandering quilt thread paths.

MAKE THE IMPROV BLOCKS

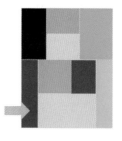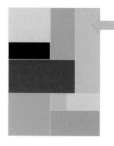

1. Start by sorting your scrap pieces into four piles according to size.

   - **Bits (smallest scraps):** squares or rectangles roughly the size of your hand, without fingers
   - **Pieces (a little larger):** squares or rectangles roughly the size of your entire hand, including fingers
   - **Strings (shorter narrow scraps):** skinny scraps that are about 12" (30.5cm) or shorter
   - **Strips (longer narrow scraps):** skinny scraps that are longer than 12" (30.5cm), up to the entire width-of-fabric

5. Sew two of the units together. Turn the units, or add additional scraps if necessary to make them fit together. Then repeat this process for the second pair of sewn units.

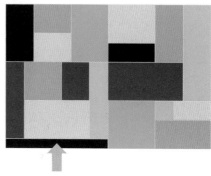

6. Sew the two units from step 5 together to make one larger improv unit. Turn the units, or add additional scraps if necessary to make them fit together. Continue adding scraps to the improv unit until it is the desired size for the quilt back. Trim the improv blocks to size if necessary.

   - **Lap size:** Make 6 blocks, 12½" x 12½" (31.8 x 31.8cm)
   - **Twin XL size:** Make 6 blocks, 18½" x 18½" (47 x 47cm)
   - **Queen size:** Make 6 blocks, 15½" x 18½" (39.4 x 47cm)

2. Choose two scraps from the pile of "bits" that are similar in length, and sew them together. Trim away any excess length. Repeat this process three times to make four pairs of sewn bits.

3. Choose a scrap from the pile of "pieces" that is the same length or slightly longer than the pair of sewn bits, and sew the piece to the side of the unit. Trim away any excess length. Repeat this process for all remaining pairs of sewn bits.

> When building the improv units, sew the scraps randomly, with some vertical seams and some horizontal seams. This gives the improv block its unique look.

4. Next, add a scrap from the strings pile to the sewn unit. Repeat this process for the remaining sewn units. At this point, each sewn unit should have four different scraps.

ASSEMBLE THE QUILT BACK

7. For the Lap size, refer to the Lap Quilt Assembly Diagram and lay out the six 12½" (31.8cm) improv blocks into one column, and sew them together to make one long improv column, 12½" x 72" (31.8 x 182.9cm).

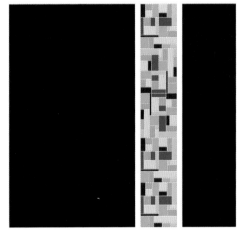

8. Then, sew the two 18" x 42" (45.7 x 106.7cm) strips of the main fabric to make one long strip measuring 18" x 84" (45.7 x 213.4cm). Sew the improv strip between the long strip and the 42" x 72" (106.7 x 182.9cm) piece of main fabric as shown, and trim away the excess length to complete the quilt back.

9. For the Twin XL size, refer to the Twin XL Quilt Assembly Diagram and lay out the six 18½" (47cm) improv blocks into one column, and sew them together to make one long improv column, 18½" x 108" (47 x 274.3cm).

10. Then, sew the three 24" x 42" (61 x 106.7cm) strips of the main fabric to make one long strip measuring 24" x 126" (61 x 320cm). Sew the improv strip between the long strip and the 42" x 108" (106.7 x 274.3cm) piece of main fabric as shown, and trim away the excess length to complete the quilt back.

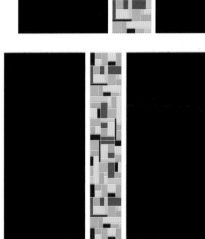

11. For the Queen size, refer to the Queen Quilt Assembly Diagram and lay out the six 15½" x 18½" (39.4 x 47cm) improv blocks into one column, and sew them together to make one long improv column, 15½" x 108" (39.4 x 274.3cm). Sew the improv column between the two 42" x 108" (106.7 x 274.3cm) lengths of main fabric to complete the quilt back.

FINISH THE QUILT

Refer to the Basting and Quilt Finishing section on page 138 for instructions on basting, quilting, and binding your quilt.

12. Layer the backing, batting, and quilt top and baste the layers together. Hand- or machine-quilt as desired.

Cool Columns

SKILL LEVEL ✳ ✳ ✳ ✳ ✳
Confident Beginner

Sometimes, when making a quilt that requires fat quarters (or quarter-yard cuts), I purposely choose many more fabrics than needed—sometimes even double! This habit adds so much interesting print variety to the front of the quilt, and it guarantees tons of leftovers to completely (or almost completely) create the quilt back. This also allows me to use up lots of the smaller cuts from my stash without having to buy yardage to "fill out" the scraps for the back.

FINISHED BACKING DIMENSIONS

Lap 63" x 75" (160 x 190.5cm)

Twin XL 84" x 105" (213.4 x 266.7cm)

Queen 105" x 105" (266.7 x 266.7cm)

The size of your backing will be based on your unique scraps and will be specific to your own quilt. As long as your backing is a few inches larger than your quilt top as discussed on page 8 in Quilt Back Basics, you don't need to worry too much about the specific size of your scraps.

This backing works best with leftover rectangles that are all the same length, and of course, large enough in size and number to cover the entire back. If your leftovers are irregular in length, or if you find that you don't have quite enough for the entire backing, the Lava Flow (page 44) or Double Bar (page 64) backings are great alternatives.

The quilt shown was made using leftover rectangles from fat quarters, each measuring 8" x 21" (20.3 x 53.3cm) long. This chart shows sizing for making a quilt backing using leftover rectangles from fat quarters or quarter-yard cuts, each measuring 21" (53.3cm) long.

Cutting All measurements include ¼" (0.5cm) seam allowances.

	Lap	Twin XL	Queen
From scraps	Trim leftover rectangles to 21" (53.3cm) wide, and straighten the edges. Rectangles may be varying lengths, as long as the length is consistent.		

Note: Seam allowances should be pressed after each join. Press open or press alternating rows/columns toward the darker fabric based on your preference.

For the corresponding quilt top, Rock Candy, see page 146.

The secret to mixing prints is pairing designs of different sizes. You can see how I generally space out the large, medium, and small prints so they each have a moment to shine.

ASSEMBLE THE QUILT BACK

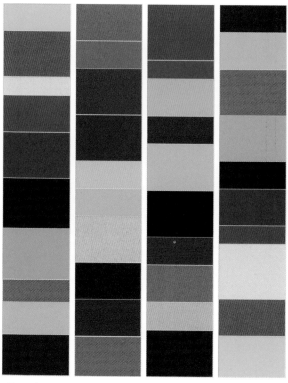

1. For the Lap size, lay out the rectangles into three columns as shown in the Lap Quilt Assembly Diagram and sew the rectangles into columns. After sewing, each column should measure 21" x 75" (53.3 x 190.5cm). Add additional rectangles to lengthen the columns or trim away any additional length as needed, and sew the columns together to complete the quilt back.

2. For the Twin XL size, lay out the rectangles into four columns as shown in the Twin XL Quilt Assembly Diagram and sew the rectangles into columns. After sewing, each column should measure 21" x 105" (53.3 x 266.7cm). Add additional rectangles to lengthen the columns or trim away any additional length as needed, and sew the columns together to complete the quilt back.

If your rectangles are shorter than 21" (53.3cm), your backing may require an additional column for adequate width. Let your scraps be your guide!

If you don't have quite enough scrap rectangles to completely fill out your columns, don't despair. It's easy to substitute one of the columns for a single coordinating fabric.

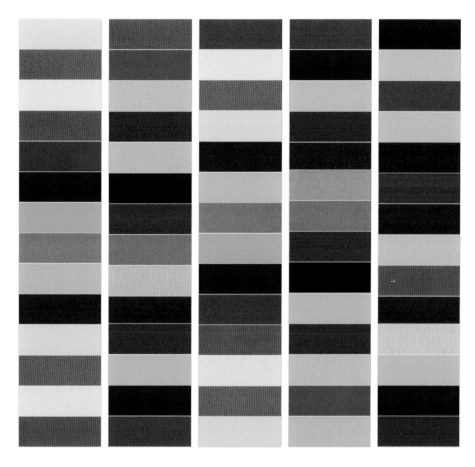

3. For the Queen size, lay out the rectangles into five columns as shown in the Queen Quilt Assembly Diagram and sew the rectangles into columns. After sewing, each column should measure 21" x 105" (53.3 x 266.7cm). Add additional rectangles to lengthen the columns or trim away any additional length as needed, and sew the columns together to complete the quilt back.

> This backing also looks great using rectangles with random lengths as shown in the Twin XL Quilt Assembly Diagram.

FINISH THE QUILT

Refer to the Basting and Quilt Finishing section on page 138 for instructions on basting, quilting, and binding your quilt.

4. Layer the backing, batting, and quilt top and baste the layers together. Hand- or machine-quilt as desired.

Long and Short

SKILL LEVEL ✳ ✳ ✳ ✳ ✳
Confident Beginner

Similar to the Cool Columns backing, a Long and Short backing is created entirely from the leftovers from the front of your quilt. But instead of using all short rectangles, the Long and Short backing makes the most of your scraps, using a combination of fat quarter rectangles and selvage-to-selvage strips measuring a full 42" (106.7cm).

FINISHED BACKING DIMENSIONS

Lap 63" x 75" (160 x 190.5cm)

Twin XL 84" x 108" (213.4 x 274.3cm)

Queen 105" x 108" (266.7 x 274.3cm)

The size of your backing will be based on your unique scraps and will be specific to your own quilt. As long as your backing is a few inches larger than your quilt top as discussed on page 8 in Quilt Back Basics, you don't need to worry too much about the specific size of your scraps.

This backing works best with rectangles that are either 21" (53.3cm) long or 42" (106.7cm) long, and of course, large enough in size and number to cover the entire back. If your leftovers are irregular in length, or if you find that you don't have quite enough for the entire backing, the Lava Flow (page 44) or Double Bar (page 64) backings are great alternatives.

The quilt shown was made using rectangles from fat quarters, each measuring 21" (53.3cm) long, and strips from yardage, 42" (106.7cm) long.

Cutting All measurements include ¼" (0.5cm) seam allowances.

	Lap	Twin XL	Queen
From scraps	Trim leftover fat quarter rectangles to 21" (53.3cm) long and straighten the edges. Trim leftover selvage-to-selvage strips to 42" (106.7cm) long and straighten the edges. Rectangles may be varying lengths, as long as the length is either 21" (53.3cm) or 42" (106.7cm).		

Note: Seam allowances should be pressed after each join. Press open or press alternating rows/columns toward the darker fabric based on your preference.

For the corresponding quilt top, Boho Beads, see page 146.

I love combining quilt fronts and backs that are almost opposite in design. While the front is symmetrical, the back is intentionally off center; while the front is balanced by a neutral background, the back is a burst of colors.

ASSEMBLE THE QUILT BACK

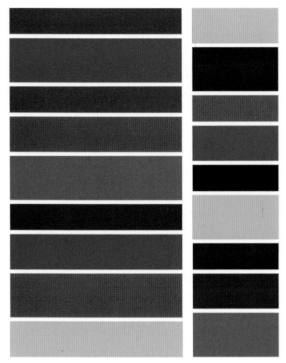

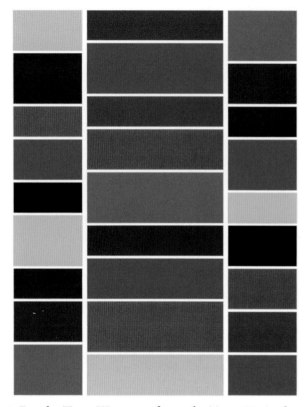

1. For the Lap size, refer to the Lap Quilt Assembly Diagram to lay out the rectangles into two columns with 42" (106.7cm) rectangles on the left, and 21" (53.3cm) rectangles on the right, and sew the rectangles into columns. Add additional rectangles to lengthen the columns to 75" (190.5cm), or trim away any additional length as needed, and sew the columns together to complete the quilt back.

2. For the Twin XL size, refer to the Twin XL Quilt Assembly Diagram to lay out the rectangles into three columns as shown, with the 42" (106.7cm) wide column in the center of two 21" (53.3cm) wide columns, and sew the rectangles together into columns. Add additional rectangles to lengthen the columns to 108" (274.3cm), or trim away any additional length as needed, and sew the columns together to complete the quilt back.

> If you need a little extra width, cut a ½ yard (45.7cm) of fabric into two lengths, each 9" x 42" (22.9 x 106.7cm), and sew them together end to end to make one long strip. Sew the long solid strip between the long and short scrap columns to make your backing 72" (182.9cm) wide!

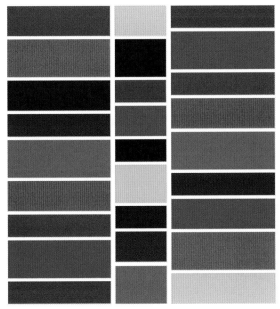

3. For the Queen size, refer to the Queen Quilt Assembly Diagram to lay out the rectangles into three columns as shown, with one 21" (53.3cm) wide column in the center of two 42" (106.7cm) wide columns, and sew the rectangles together into columns. Add additional rectangles to lengthen the columns to 108" (274.3cm), or trim away any additional length as needed, and sew the columns together to complete the quilt back.

FINISH THE QUILT

Refer to the Basting and Quilt Finishing section on page 138 for instructions on basting, quilting, and binding your quilt.

4. Layer the backing, batting, and quilt top and baste the layers together. Hand- or machine-quilt as desired.

The Long and Short quilt back is a great use for leftover strips.

When working with scraps of various widths, your seams will not always "meet up," and that's okay! The end result is still beautiful.

Lava Flow

SKILL LEVEL ✳ ✳ ✳ ✳ ✳
Confident Beginner

Sometimes cutting the pieces for the front of your quilt doesn't leave you with rectangles that are a consistent length, and sometimes you just don't have enough scraps to cover the entire back of your quilt. The Lava Flow design is a perfect backing choice if you find yourself with a hodgepodge of scrap rectangles!

FINISHED BACKING DIMENSIONS
Lap 72" x 72" (182.9 x 182.9cm)

Twin XL 84" x 108" (213.4 x 274.3cm)

Queen 100" x 108" (254 x 274.3cm)

The size of your backing will be based on your unique scraps and will be specific to your own quilt. As long as your backing is a few inches larger than your quilt top as discussed on page 8 in Quilt Back Basics, you don't need to worry too much about the specific size of your scraps.

Materials Yardage is based on 42" (106.7cm) wide fabric.

This quilt back requires scrap rectangles that are various sizes, with background fabric to fill out the backing. The chart below gives a generous approximation of background yardage required, however, if you have fewer scraps, your backing may require more.

	Lap	Twin XL	Queen
Scrap Rectangles	Scraps may be any length and any width		
Background Fabric	Approximately 2½ yards (2.3m)	Approximately 3¾ yards (3.4m)	Approximately 4½ yards (4.1m)

SORT YOUR SCRAPS
Sort your scraps into piles of similar length. The length of each scrap rectangle within each pile doesn't need to be exactly the same, but they should be similar to each other. They may be any width. In each pile, take note of the rectangle that is *the shortest*, and put it on top of the pile.

Cutting All measurements include ¼" (0.5cm) seam allowances.

	Lap	Twin XL	Queen
Scraps	Trim the rectangles in each pile to the shortest rectangle in the pile. Rectangles may be varying widths, as long as the length of each pile is consistent. Note the length of the rectangles in each pile.		
Background Fabric	Cut 1 strip, 42" (106.7cm) long, the exact length of the rectangles for each pile. Set the remaining background fabric aside.		

Note: Seam allowances should be pressed after each join. Press open or press alternating rows/columns toward the darker fabric based on your preference.

The Lava Flow backing is beautiful with this limited palette, and I was able to pull scraps in these colors from my bin to round it out. However, this design can still work even with a wide variety of color. Just use the color palette of your quilt as a guide and it's sure to look amazing!

ASSEMBLE THE QUILT BACK

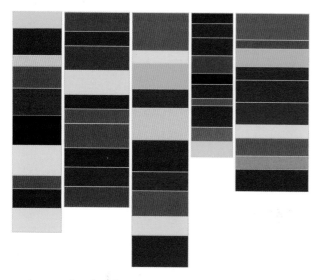

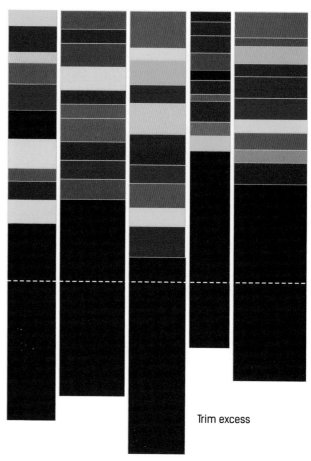

Trim excess

1. Sew each pile of scrap rectangles into a column. Each column should be shorter than the full length of the quilt back. If there are more rectangles than needed in a single column, divide them into two columns.

If you would rather do a little math, you can measure the length of your scrap columns and cut background rectangles to the exact length needed to make each column 72" (182.9cm) long!

2. For the Lap size, refer to the Quilt Assembly Diagram, to sew a 42" (106.7cm) background strip *of the same width* to the end of each scrap column. Trim each column to 72" (182.9cm), or add an additional rectangle of background fabric to increase the length to 72" (182.9cm), and then sew the columns together to complete the quilt back.

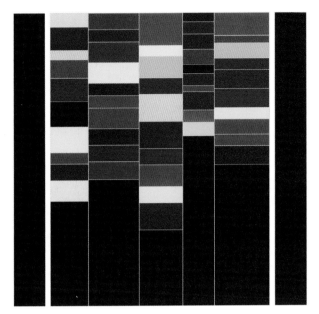

3. Measure the width of the quilt back and determine if extra width is needed. If your quilt back measures less than 72" (182.9cm), add an additional column if you have more scraps, OR add a strip of background fabric to each side to widen the back to 72" (182.9cm).

4. For the Twin XL and Queen sizes, use the same process in steps 1–2, but each column should measure 108" (274.3cm) long.

5. For the Twin XL size, measure the width of the quilt back and determine if extra width is needed. If your quilt back is less than 84" (213.4cm), add an additional column if you have more scraps, OR add a strip of background fabric to each side to widen the back to 84" (213.4cm). The finished quilt back should measure 84" x 108" (213.4 x 274.3cm).

6. For the Queen size, measure the width of the quilt back and determine if extra width is needed. If your quilt back measures less than 100" (254cm), add an additional column if you have more scraps. Alternatively, you may add a strip of background fabric to each side to widen the back to 100" (254cm). The finished quilt back should measure 100" x 108" (254 x 274.3cm).

FINISH THE QUILT

Refer to the Basting and Quilt Finishing section on page 138 for instructions on basting, quilting, and binding your quilt.

7. Layer the backing, batting, and quilt top and baste the layers together. Hand- or machine-quilt as desired.

Railroad

When the leftovers from my quilt are entirely made up of full selvage-to-selvage strips, I love to make a Railroad quilt back. Leaving those strips uncut utilizes their entire length to make up the main section of your backing, resulting in a backing with lots of wow factor!

FINISHED BACKING DIMENSIONS

Lap 78" x 78" (198.1 x 198.1cm)

Twin XL 90" x 104" (228.6 x 264.2cm)

Queen 102" x 104" (259.1 x 264.2cm)

Materials Yardage is based on 42" (106.7cm) wide fabric.

This backing requires leftover strips that are 42" (106.7cm) long, and of course, enough to cover the entire length of your quilt. If you have a mix of 42" (106.7cm) strips and 21" (53.3cm) rectangles (from fat quarters), try the Long and Short backing instead.

	Lap	Twin XL	Queen
Scrap Strips, 42" (106.7cm) long	Enough strips to cover the entire length of the quilt back.		
Three coordinating prints for the vertical side strips	¾ yard (68.6cm) each	1¼ yard (1.1m) each	1½ yards (1.4m) each

Cutting All measurements include ¼" (0.5cm) seam allowances.

	Lap	Twin XL	Queen
From scraps	Trim leftover yardage strips to 42" (106.7cm) and straighten the edges. Strips may be varying widths, as long as the length is 42" (106.7cm).		
Side fabrics, From each	4 strips, 6½" x 42" (16.5 x 106.7cm)	5 strips, 8½" x 42" (21.6 x 106.7cm), subcut from one strip, 2 rectangles, 8½" x 21" (21.6 x 53.3cm)	5 strips, 10½" x 42" (26.7 x 106.7cm), subcut from one strip, 2 rectangles, 10½" x 21" (26.7 x 53.3cm)

Note: Seam allowances should be pressed after each join. Press open or press alternating rows/columns toward the darker fabric based on your preference.

For the corresponding quilt top, Filigree, see page 146.

Strip piecing on a grand scale couldn't be easier. The Railroad quilt back joins varying strip widths, alternating the yellows and blues from the quilt front yardage for a horizontal strip center, then borders each side with the mirror image of vertical strips from three prints. This is one where you'll want to plan ahead to make sure you purchase enough extra yardage.

ASSEMBLE THE QUILT BACK

1. For all sizes, lay out the 42" (106.7cm) strips, and then sew them together to make one large scrap strip set for the center of the quilt back. The strip set should be long enough to cover the entire quilt back.

If you don't have quite enough scrap strips and need a little extra length, that's okay! Add an extra strip of one of your side fabrics to the top and bottom to make it long enough.

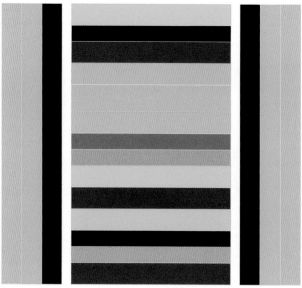

2. For the Lap size, lay out two 6½" x 42" (16.5 x 106.7cm) strips of one side fabric and sew them together, end to end, to make one long strip, 6½" x 84" (16.5 x 213.4cm). Refer to the Lap Quilt Assembly Diagram, and sew the long strip to the right side of the strip set. Trim away the excess length from the side strip. Repeat this process on the left side of the strip set.

3. Use the same process to make two 6½" x 84" (16.5 x 213.4cm) long strips from each of the second and third side fabrics, and sew them to the sides of the strip set as shown to complete the quilt back.

4. For the Twin XL size, lay out two 8½" x 42" (21.6 x 106.7cm) strips, plus one 8½" x 21" (21.6 x 53.3cm) rectangle of one side fabric and sew them together, end to end, to make one long strip, 8½" x 104" (21.6 x 264.2cm). Refer to the Twin XL Quilt Assembly Diagram, and sew the long strip to the right side of the strip set. Repeat this process on the left side of the strip set.

5. Use the same process to make two 8½" x 104" (21.6 x 264.2cm) long strips from each of the second and third side fabrics, and sew them to the sides of the strip set as shown to complete the quilt back.

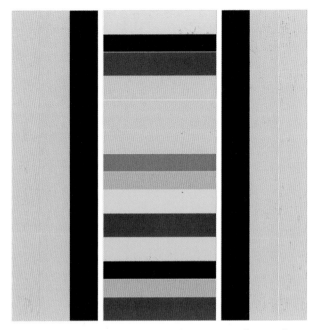

6. For the Queen size, lay out two 10½" x 42" (26.7 x 106.7cm) strips, plus one 10½" x 21" (26.7 x 53.3cm) rectangle of one side fabric and sew them together, end to end, to make one long strip, 10½" x 104" (26.7 x 264.2cm). Refer to the Queen Quilt Assembly Diagram, and sew the long strip to the right side of the strip set. Repeat this process on the left side of the strip set.

7. Use the same process to make two 10½" x 104" (26.7 x 264.2cm) long strips from each of the second and third side fabrics, and sew them to the sides of the strip set as shown to complete the quilt back.

FINISH THE QUILT

Refer to Basting and Quilt Finishing section on page 138 for instructions on basting, quilting, and binding your quilt.

8. Layer the backing, batting, and quilt top and baste the layers together. Hand- or machine-quilt as desired.

Bar Graph

SKILL LEVEL ✳ ✳ ✳ ✳ ✳
Confident Beginner

If you have just a few leftover scrap strips, a Bar Graph back is a great place to show them off. Since this design utilizes scraps with different lengths, you don't need to worry if you don't have full selvage-to-selvage strips.

FINISHED BACKING DIMENSIONS

Lap 70" x 70" (177.8 x 177.8cm)

Twin XL 82" x 102" (208.3 x 259.1cm)

Queen 94" x 102" (238.8 x 259.1cm)

Materials Yardage is based on 42" (106.7cm) wide fabric.

	Lap	Twin XL	Queen
Non-directional Main Fabric	3½ yards (3.2m)	5¼ yards (4.8m)	6¼ yards (5.7m)
Scraps	7 leftover strips and rectangles, from 15" to 42" (38.1 to 106.7cm) long. OR scrap strips and rectangles of various width, totaling 42" (106.7cm) wide (after accounting for seam allowance)	11 leftover strips and rectangles, from 15" to 42" (38.1 to 106.7 cm) long. OR scrap strips and rectangles of various width, totaling 66" (167.7 cm) wide (after accounting for seam allowance)	

The quilt shown uses scrap strips of various length, but a consistent 6½" (16.5cm) wide. If your scraps are various widths, you can still make a Bar Graph backing! Just be sure you have enough for the total length of the quilt *after accounting for seam allowance*. For example, the quilt shown uses seven strips that *finish* at 6" (15.2cm), for a total of 42" (106.7cm). As long as you have 42" (106.7cm) of total scrap width for the lap size, or 66" (167.6cm) of total scrap width for the Twin and Queen sizes, the backing will look great! The background fabric requirements listed below allow a little extra fabric to account for scraps of various width and length.

Cutting All measurements include ¼" (0.5cm) seam allowances.

The cutting chart gives instructions for using 6½" (16.5cm) wide scrap strips, as well as using scrap strips in various widths.

	Lap	Twin XL	Queen
From scraps	Trim scrap strips and rectangles to 6½" (16.5cm) wide, and leave them at their full length. OR leave the scrap width and length as-is, but straighten the edges		
From Main Fabric	6 strips, 3½" x 42" (9 x 106.7cm) 1 strip, 29" x 42" (73.7 x 106.7cm), subcut 6 rectangles, 3½" x 29" (9 x 73.7cm)(yields 6 extra) 4 strips, 5½" x 42" (14 x 106.7cm) 7 strips, 6½" x 42" (16.5 x 106.7cm)	12 strips, 3½" x 42" (9 x 106.7cm)1 strip, 29" x 42" (73.7 x 106.7cm), subcut 12 rectangles, 3½" x 29" (9 x 73.7cm) 3 strips, 12½" x 42" (31.8 x 106.7cm) 11 strips, 6½" x 42" (16.5 x 106.7cm)	12 strips, 3½" x 42" (9 x 106.7cm) 1 strip, 29" x 42" (73.7 x 106.7cm), subcut 12 rectangles, 3½" x 29" (9 x 73.7cm) 3 strips, 24½" x 42" (62.2 x 106.7cm) 11 strips, 6½" x 42" (16.5 x 106.7cm)
	OR if using scrap strips of varying width: Cut 1 strip of main fabric for each of your scraps strips and rectangles, 42" (106.7cm) long x the exact width of each scrap strip		

Note: Seam allowances should be pressed after each join. Press open or press alternating rows/columns toward the darker fabric based on your preference.

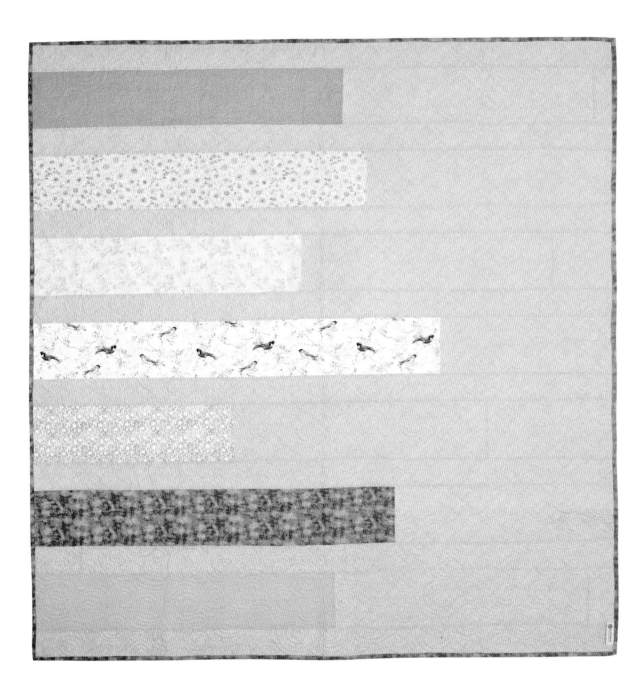

The prints strips are featured so prominently in this design! Using a non-directional main fabric will help you make the most of your yardage and really allow those scrap strips take center stage.

MAKE THE SASHING

1. For all sizes, sew one 3½" x 42" (8.9 x 106.7cm) strip and one 3½" x 29" (8.9 x 73.7cm) strip together, end to end to make one sashing strip, 3½" x 70" (8.9 x 177.8cm). Repeat this process to make the sashing strips for the entire quilt.

   - **Lap:** Make 6 strips.

   - **Twin XL:** Make 12 strips.

   - **Queen:** Make 12 strips.

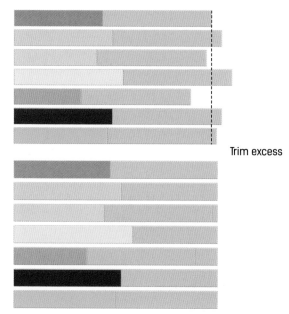

Trim excess

ASSEMBLE THE QUILT BACK

2. For the Lap size, lay out the seven scrap strips in the desired order. Then sew one scrap strip and one 6½" (16.5cm) background strip together, end-to-end to make one long strip. Repeat this process for all scrap strips.

3. Adjust the sewn strips from left to right if necessary to create the bar graph effect, with each strip ending in a random place.

Remember! You can use the same piecing method with scraps that are not consistent width. Just be sure your strips are 70" (177.8cm) long.

4. Measure the *longest strip* and trim it to 70" (177.8cm) long, or add an additional rectangle of background fabric to make it 70" (177.8cm) long. Use this strip as a guide to cut each of the remaining strips 70" (177.8cm) long. Or, add additional background rectangles to lengthen each strip to 70" (177.8cm) long as needed.

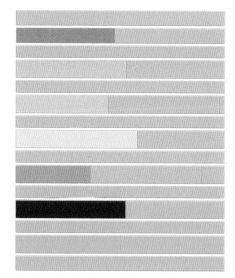

5. Refer to the Lap Quilt Assembly Diagram to lay out the trimmed bar graph strips with a 3½" x 70" (8.9 x 177.8cm) sashing strip between each, and sew the strips together. Then, sew two 5½" x 42" (14 x 106.7cm) strips together, end to end to make one long sashing strip, and sew it to the top of the quilt. Trim the excess length, and repeat this process on the bottom of the quilt to complete the quilt back.

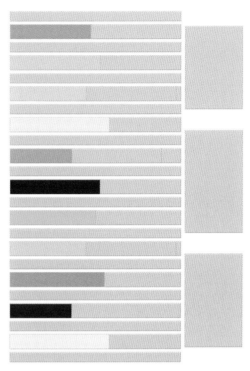

6. For the Twin XL size, use the process in steps 1–3 to make 11 bar graph strips, 6½" x 70" (16.5 x 177.8cm). Refer to the Twin XL Quilt Assembly Diagram and lay out the bar graph strips with 3½" x 70" (8.9 x 177.8cm) sashing strips between each, *and* at the top and bottom. Sew the strips together. Then sew three 12½" x 42" (31.8 x 106.7cm) background strips together, end to end to make one long strip, 12½" x 126" (31.8 x 320cm). Sew the long strip to the right side of the strip set and trim the excess length to complete the quilt back.

7. For the Queen size, use the process in steps 1–3 to make 11 bar graph strips, 6½" x 70" (16.5 x 177.8cm). Refer to the Queen Quilt Assembly Diagram and lay out the bar graph strips with 3½" x 70" (8.9 x 177.8cm) sashing strips between each, *and* at the top and bottom. Sew the strips together. Then sew three 24½" x 42" (62.2 x 106.7cm) background strips together, end to end to make one long strip, 24½" x 126" (62.2 x 320cm). Sew the long strip to the right side of the strip set and trim the excess length to complete the quilt back.

FINISH THE QUILT

Refer to the Basting and Quilt Finishing section on page 138 for instructions on basting, quilting, and binding your quilt.

8. Layer the backing, batting, and quilt top and baste the layers together. Hand- or machine-quilt as desired.

Chunky

SKILL LEVEL ✳ ✳ ✳ ✳ ✳
Confident Beginner

The Chunky backing is a fantastic backing choice for large leftover pieces, even if no two are the same size. For this backing, it really doesn't matter what size pieces are used. In fact, you won't even need to measure them! I always refer to these scraps as chunks, and a chunky improv backing is much easier than you think!

FINISHED BACKING DIMENSIONS

It's important to note that no two Chunky backings will be alike, and that's what makes it so fun. The size of your backing will be based on your unique scraps and will be specific to your own quilt. Just make the backing a few inches larger than your quilt top as discussed on page 8 in Quilt Back Basics.

Materials

	Lap	Twin XL	Queen
Scraps	Leftover chunks of fabric, enough to cover the entire quilt back.		

Cutting

	Lap	Twin XL	Queen
Scraps	Straighten the edges of all leftover scrap chunks. Chunks may be any size, and no measurements are necessary.		

Note: Seam allowances should be pressed after each join. Press open or press alternating rows/columns toward the darker fabric based on your preference.

For the corresponding quilt top, Stems and Stones, see page 146.

Don't be discouraged by its random look. The Chunky
quilt back is easier than you think!

SORT YOUR CHUNKS

Sort the leftover chunks into piles with similar sizes. I like to sort my chunks into four piles: Large, Squares, Small Squares, Short Rectangles, and Long Rectangles.

- **Large Squares.** These pieces will likely be the largest of your leftover pieces. They may be slightly smaller than a fat quarter, or you may even choose to add an extra full fat quarter to your backing. These pieces are square, or almost square.

- **Small Squares.** As the name suggests, these pieces are smaller, and square or almost square. Because they are smaller, these chunks can easily be used as filler pieces, or sewn together to make a long row.

- **Short Rectangles.** These are rectangles that are roughly the length of a fat quarter but narrower, so they are more rectangular in shape.

- **Long Rectangles.** These rectangles are long, almost the entire width of fabric from selvage-to-selvage, or slightly shorter.

Remember that your scraps will dictate your own sorting method. Whatever chunks you have available will work!

ASSEMBLE THE QUILT BACK

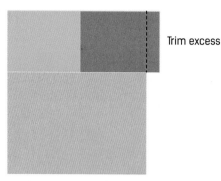

Trim excess

1. Choose one large square chunk. Then, choose smaller chunks (either rectangles or squares), and lay them out along one side of the large square. The width of the smaller chunks should be equal to the large square, or slightly longer. Sew the smaller chunks together, and then sew them to the large square as shown. Trim away any excess length.

> Always make sure that the pieces being added are long enough to cover the entire side of the sewn unit. This ensures that any necessary trimming will only be from the added piece.

2. Add another chunk to any side to make the unit larger, and trim away any excess length. Set this unit aside.

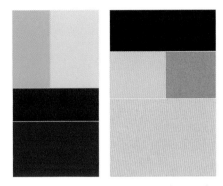

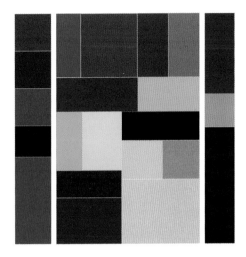

3. Repeat steps 1 and 2, starting with another large square chunk. Keep adding smaller or longer chunks to make this entire unit the same length or slightly longer than the unit created in step 2. Then sew the two units together and trim away any excess length.

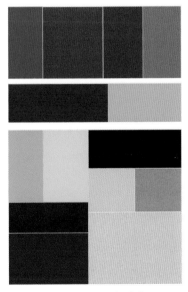

4. Repeat this process as needed, laying out and sewing chunks to the top of the unit to make the backing long enough. Fill in the length with any size chunk needed.

5. Once the back is long enough, measure the width of the unit to determine how much additional width is needed to complete the back. Refer to the Quilt Assembly Diagram to lay out narrow chunks and sew them together to make one long strip. Then attach it to the side of the main unit as shown. Repeat this process on the other side to complete the quilt back. If more width is needed, continue to add long, narrow strips to widen to the desired width.

FINISH THE QUILT

Refer to the Basting and Quilt Finishing section on page 138 for instructions on basting, quilting, and binding your quilt.

6. Layer the backing, batting, and quilt top and baste the layers together. Hand- or machine-quilt as desired.

> The size backing you need will determine how many improv chunk units you will need to make. After sewing the units together, measure them and determine how much additional length is needed to complete the quilt back. Continue to add units to make the backing long enough for your quilt.

Woven

SKILL LEVEL ✳ ✳ ✳ ✳ ✳
Confident Beginner

The Woven quilt back is a perfect choice if you have leftover strips from the front of your quilt. Whether they're consistent in size or different widths, sewing your strips into blocks keeps them organized and helps your scraps take center stage in this backing.

FINISHED BACKING DIMENSIONS

Lap 68" x 68" (172.7 x 172.7cm)

Twin XL 80" x 108" (203.2 x 274.3cm)

Queen 100" x 108" (254 x 274.3cm)

Materials Yardage is based on 42" (106.7cm) wide fabric.

	Lap	Twin XL	Queen
Scrap strips	Leftover strips sewn into 20½" (52.1cm) blocks as shown in step 1.		
Background fabric	2 yards (1.8m)	4 yards (3.7m)	4¾ yards (4.3m)

Cutting All measurements include ¼" (0.5cm) seam allowances.

	Lap	Twin XL	Queen
From the background fabric, cut	4 strips, 14½" x 42" (36.8 x 106.7cm) 2 strips, 4½" x 42" (11.4 x 106.7cm)	4 strips, 34" x 42" (86.4 x 106.7cm)	5 strips, 34" x 42" (86.4 x 106.7cm), subcut from one strip 2 rectangles, 16½" x 34" (41.9 x 86.4cm)

Note: Seam allowances should be pressed after each join. Press open or press alternating rows/columns toward the darker fabric based on your preference.

For the corresponding quilt top, Birthstones, see page 146.

The Woven quilt back is very linear, making it a great contrast for the hexagon shaped jewels on the front of this quilt. Though this quilt exclusively uses solids, it would also look amazing with prints.

MAKE THE SCRAP BLOCKS

1. Lay out the scrap strips for the block and sew the block together as shown. Add additional strips or trim the block as necessary to make a block measuring 20½" (52.1cm) square.

- **Lap:** Make six blocks
- **Twin XL:** Make eight blocks
- **Queen:** Make ten blocks

The quilt shown uses leftover strips from fat quarters and yardage, so they were easily trimmed to 20½" (52.1cm) long. If your strips are shorter or narrower, don't worry! Just sew shorter strips end to end to make them 20½" (52.1cm) long. Or, you can make your scrap blocks a completely different size. It's easy to adjust the width of the background strips to accommodate your unique scraps!

| Consistent length and width | Different widths | Random length and width |

ASSEMBLE THE QUILT BACK

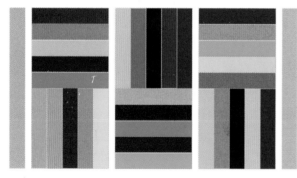

2. Refer to the Lap Quilt Assembly Diagram to lay out the blocks into two rows with three blocks in each row, alternating the direction of the strips to create the woven effect. Sew the blocks into rows and sew the rows together as shown. Then, sew a 4½" x 42" (11.4 x 106.7cm) background strip to the beginning and end of the block unit to make a center unit measuring 40½" x 68½" (102.9 x 174cm). Trim the excess length from the background strips.

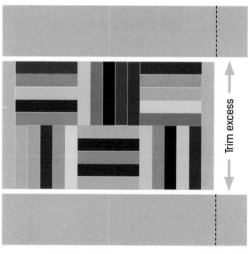

Trim excess

3a. Sew two 14½" x 42" (36.8 x 106.7cm) background strips end to end to make one long strip measuring 14½" x 84" (36.8 x 213.4cm), and sew it to the top of the center unit.

Remember! Your backing will always be larger than the quilt top. As this quilt shows, those side background strips may get trimmed away during the basting step, and that's okay!

3b. Repeat this process to make a second long background strip and sew it to the bottom of the center unit. Trim the excess length from the background strips to complete the backing.

4a. Refer to the Twin XL Quilt Assembly Diagram to lay out the blocks into two rows, with four blocks in each row and sew them together as shown to make the center unit. Then, sew two 34½" x 42" (87.6 x 106.7cm) background strips together, end-to-end to make one long strip, measuring 34½" x 84" (87.6 x 213.4cm) and sew it to the top of the center unit.

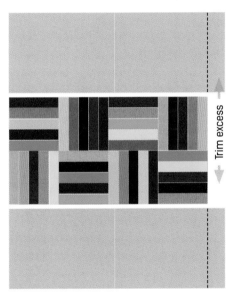

4b. Repeat this process to make a second long background strip and sew it to the bottom of the block unit. Trim the excess length from the background strips to complete the backing.

5a. Refer to the Queen Quilt Assembly Diagram to lay out the blocks into two rows, with five blocks in each row and sew them together as shown to make the center unit. Then, sew two 34½" x 42" (87.6 x 106.7cm) background strips, plus one 16½" x 34" (41.9 x 86.4cm) background rectangle together, end-to-end to make one long strip, measuring 34½" x 100" (87.6 x 254cm) and sew it to the top of the center unit.

For a little extra flair, choose an additional coordinating fabric for the two 16½" x 34" (41.9 x 86.4cm) rectangles and sew them between the two lengths of the main background fabric.

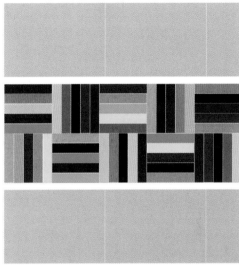

5b. Repeat this process to make a second long background strip and sew it to the bottom of the center unit. Trim the excess length from the background strips to complete the backing.

FINISH THE QUILT

Refer to the Basting and Quilt Finishing section on page 138 for instructions on basting, quilting, and binding your quilt.

6. Layer the backing, batting, and quilt top and baste the layers together. Hand- or machine-quilt as desired.

Double Bar

SKILL LEVEL ✳ ✳ ✳ ✳ ✳
Confident Beginner

If you have some bigger rectangles from fat quarters or yardage, along with some smaller scrap pieces, show them off in the Double Bar quilt back. Don't add those smaller pieces to your scrap bins. Both will look great together in this backing!

FINISHED BACKING DIMENSIONS

Lap 72" x 72" (182.9 x 182.9cm)

Twin XL 80" x 108" (203.2 x 274.3cm)

Queen 96" x 108" (243.8 x 274.3cm)

This backing requires leftover strips that are either 21" (53.3cm) or 42" (106.7cm) long, along with some smaller pieces, and of course, enough to cover the entire length of your quilt. If your scraps are shorter than required but you still want to make a Double Bar backing, increase the width of the bars to make the backing wide enough. If you only have enough leftovers for a single column, try the Walking Path backing, and showcase those scraps in the center stripe!

Materials Yardage is based on 42" (106.7cm) wide fabric.

	Lap	Twin XL	Queen
Large scrap rectangles, 21" or 42" (53.3 or 106.7cm) long	Enough strips to cover the entire length of the quilt back in two full columns. Scraps may be various widths.		
Smaller scrap rectangles	Enough pieces to cover the entire length of the quilt back.		
	At least 6½" (16.5cm) long Scrap pieces may be varying widths, but should be at least 6½" (16.5cm) long.	At least 8½" (21.6cm) long Scrap pieces may be varying widths, but should be at least 8½" (21.6cm) long.	At least 12½" (31.8cm) long Scrap pieces may be varying widths, but should be at least 12½" (31.8cm) long.
Double Bar fabric	1½ yards (1.4m)	2⅔ yards (2.4m)	3 yards (2.7m)

Cutting All measurements include ¼" (0.5cm) seam allowances.

	Lap	Twin XL	Queen
Large scrap rectangles	Trim any leftover 42" (106.7cm) strips to 21" (53.3cm) long, and straighten the edges of all large scraps. Rectangles may be varying widths, as long as the length is 21" (53.3cm)		
Smaller scrap rectangles	Trim all small scraps to 6½" (16.5cm) long, and straighten the edges. Scraps may be varying widths, as long as the length is 6½" (16.5cm).	Trim all small scraps to 8½" (21.6cm) long, and straighten the edges. Scraps may be varying widths, as long as the length is 8½" (21.6cm).	Trim all small scraps to 12½" (31.8cm) long, and straighten the edges. Scraps may be varying widths, as long as the length is 12½" (31.8cm).
Double Bar fabric	4 strips, 12½" x 42" (31.8 x 106.7cm)	6 strips, 15½" x 42" (39.4 x 106.7cm)	From the 3 yard piece, subcut 2 lengths, 21" x 108" (53.3 x 274.3cm)

Note: Seam allowances should be pressed after each join. Press open or press alternating rows/columns toward the darker fabric based on your preference.

For the corresponding quilt top, Baubles, see page 146.

Notice that small scraps are used in the center column, but
they're pieced together to fill out the side columns as well.
The benefit to these quilt designs is that they can easily
be adjusted depending on the size of your scraps.

ASSEMBLE THE QUILT BACK

1. For all sizes, lay out the 21" (53.3cm) scrap rectangles into two columns. Sew the rectangles together to complete two large scrap columns for the right and left side of the quilt back. Each large scrap column should be long enough to cover the entire length of the quilt back.

2. For all sizes, lay out the small scrap pieces into a single column, and sew the pieces together to complete the small scrap column for the center of the quilt back. The small scrap column should be long enough to cover the entire length of the quilt back.

If your heart is set on a Double Bar quilt back, but you don't have quite enough scrap rectangles, add a little extra background fabric to fill it out!

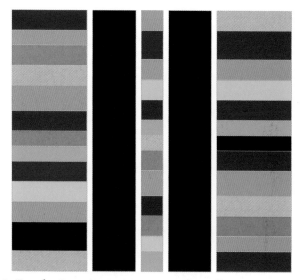

3. For the Lap size, sew two 12½" x 42" (31.8 x 106.7cm) strips of the double bar fabric end to end to make one double bar strip measuring 12½" x 84" (31.8 x 213.4cm). Make two double bar strips. Refer to the Lap Quilt Assembly Diagram to lay out the large scrap columns, the double bar strips, and the small scrap column in order as shown. Sew the columns together. Then trim away the excess length from the double bar strips to complete the quilt back.

Many quilters stick to neutral color thread, but experimenting can be fun! The quilt shown is finished with bright coral thread, which gives it another layer of interest.

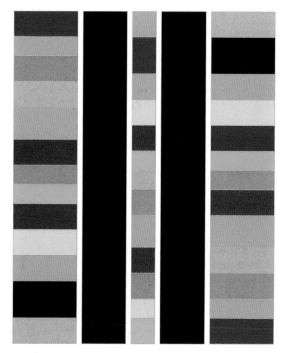

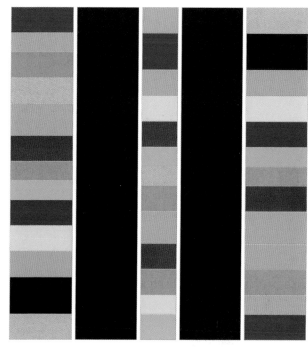

4. For the Twin XL size, sew three 15½" x 42" (39.4 x 106.7cm) strips of the double bar fabric end to end to make one double bar strip measuring 15½" x 126" (39.4 x 320cm). Make two double bar strips. Refer to the Twin XL Quilt Assembly Diagram to lay out the large scrap columns, the double bar strips, and the small scrap column in order as shown. Sew the columns together. Then trim away the excess length from the double bar strips to complete the quilt back.

If you have lots of vibrant colors and prints, choosing a darker shade for the double bars can give your eye a place to rest. The solid navy fabric in this Double Bar quilt back is the perfect choice for calming these bright fabrics.

5. For the Queen size, refer to the Queen Quilt Assembly Diagram to lay out the large scrap columns, the 21" x 108" (53.3 x 274.3cm) double bar strips, and the small scrap column in order as shown. Sew the columns together to complete the quilt back.

FINISH THE QUILT

Refer to the Basting and Quilt Finishing section on page 138 for instructions on basting, quilting, and binding your quilt.

6. Layer the backing, batting, and quilt top and baste the layers together. Hand- or machine-quilt as desired.

Around the Corner

SKILL LEVEL ✳ ✳ ✳ ✳ ✳
Confident Beginner

I don't know many quilters who don't have a stash of fabric just waiting to be added to a quilt. When you pull fabrics from your stash for a quilt, it stands to reason that your leftovers may be completely random in size. You might have a large piece of yardage, a few strips of fabric that are a full selvage-to-selvage length, and even some pieces of fat quarters. Just because your scraps aren't a consistent size doesn't mean they can't come together to make a special backing.

FINISHED BACKING DIMENSIONS

Lap 63" x 75" (160 x 190.5cm)

Twin XL 81" x 105" (205.7 x 266.7cm)

Queen 99" x 105" (251.5 x 266.7cm)

Materials Yardage is based on 42" (106.7cm) wide fabric.

	Lap	Twin XL	Queen
Main print	1 yard (91.4cm)	1½ yards (1.4m)	1½ yards (1.4m)
Scraps	Leftover pieces from fat quarters, 21" (53.3cm) long, and leftover pieces from yardage, 42" (106.7cm) long		

Cutting All measurements include ¼" (0.5cm) seam allowances.

	Lap	Twin XL	Queen
From scraps	Trim leftover rectangles to 21" (53.3cm) long or 42" (106.7cm) long, and straighten the edges. Rectangles may be varying widths, as long as the length is consistent.		

Note: Seam allowances should be pressed after each join. Press open or press alternating rows/columns toward the darker fabric based on your preference.

> The main "corner" fabric is a wonderful place to show off a large statement fabric. You might be hesitant to cut the prints in these kinds of fabrics because they're so big and beautiful. Luckily, with an Around the Corner quilt back, you don't have to!

For the corresponding quilt top, Bubble Bath, see page 146.

If you're having trouble deciding on a color palette for a quilt, start with a focus fabric or two! For this quilt, I started with two gorgeous large prints and built my color palette around them using fabrics from my stash.

ASSEMBLE THE QUILT BACK

 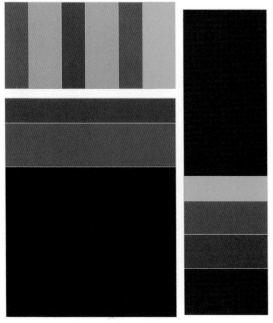

1. For the Lap size, lay out 42" (106.7cm) scrap strips and sew them together to make one large strip section, measuring 18½" x 42" (45.7 x 106.7cm). Then, sew the strip section to the top of the main piece of fabric as shown. The unit should measure 42" x 54" (106.7 x 137.1cm). After sewing the yardage strip section, any extra strips may be trimmed to 21" (53.3cm) long for later use.

If you don't have enough leftover 21" (53.3cm) strips to go all the way "around the corner," that's okay! Choose a coordinating 21" piece of "filler" fabric as shown in this quilt, or add a couple of fat quarters.

2. Lay out 21" (53.3cm) scrap strips and sew them together to make one long strip set, 21" x 42" (53.3 x 106.7cm). Sew the strip set to the top of the unit created in step 1 as shown. Then lay out and sew rectangle and 21" (53.3cm) strips to make a second long strip measuring 21" x 75" (53.3 x 190.5cm). Sew the second strip to the right side of the unit to complete the quilt back.

3. For the Twin XL size, lay out 42" (106.7cm) scrap strips and sew them together to make one large strip section, measuring 30½" x 42" (77.5 x 106.7cm). Then, sew the strip section to the top of the main piece of fabric as shown. The unit should measure 42" x 84" (106.7 x 213.4cm).

4. Lay out and sew additional 42" (106.7cm) strips to make two strip sets, 18" x 42" (45.7 x 106.7cm). Sew the strip sets together, end to end, to make one double strip set measuring 18" x 84" (45.7 x 213.4cm) and sew the double strip set strip to the right side of the unit. After sewing the double strip sections, any leftover strips may be trimmed to 21" (53.3cm) long for later use.

5. Lay out 21" (53.3cm) scrap strips and sew them together to make one long strip, 21" x 60" (53.3 x 152.4cm) and sew the strip to the top of the unit as shown. Then lay out and sew rectangle and 21" (53.3cm) strips to make a second long strip measuring 21" x 105" (53.3 x 266.7cm). Sew the second strip to the right side of the unit to complete the quilt back.

6. For the Queen size, lay out 42" (106.7cm) scrap strips and sew them together to make one large strip section, measuring 30½" x 42" (77.5 x 106.7cm). Then, sew the strip section to the top of the main piece of fabric as shown. The unit should measure 42" x 84" (106.7 x 213.4cm).

7. Lay out and sew additional 42" (106.7cm) strips to make two strip sets, 36" x 42" (91.4 x 106.7cm). Sew the strip sets together, end to end, to make one double strip set measuring 36" x 84" (91.4 x 213.4cm) and sew the double strip set to the right side of the unit. After sewing the double strip set, any leftover strips may be trimmed to 21" (53.3cm) long for later use.

8. Lay out 21" (53.3cm) scrap strips and sew them together to make one long strip, 21" x 78" (53.3 x 198.1cm) and sew the strip to the top of the unit as shown. Then lay out and sew rectangle and 21" (53.3cm) strips to make a second long strip measuring 21" x 105" (53.3 x 266.7cm). Sew the second strip to the right side of the unit to complete the quilt back.

FINISH THE QUILT

Refer to the Basting and Quilt Finishing section on page 138 for instructions on basting, quilting, and binding your quilt.

9. Layer the backing, batting, and quilt top and baste the layers together. Hand- or machine-quilt as desired.

Liberated Logs

SKILL LEVEL ✳ ✳ ✳ ✳ ✳
Confident Beginner

Log Cabin blocks are one of the oldest quilt blocks in existence, and they have so many great uses. Scrap strips of various widths are put together in this quilt back to create giant log cabin blocks, giving a new twist on a traditional favorite!

FINISHED BACKING DIMENSIONS

Lap 72" x 74" (182.9 x 188cm)

Twin XL 81" x 108" (205.7 x 274.3cm)

Queen 93" x 108" (236.2 x 274.3cm)

Materials Yardage is based on 42" (106.7cm) wide fabric.

	Lap	Twin XL	Queen
Scrap strips of various length and width for the blocks	Enough scraps for 3 blocks, each approximately 21" (53.3cm) square	Enough scraps for 4 blocks, each approximately 21" (53.3cm) square	
Non-directional fabric for the background	3 yards (2.7m)	5 yards (4.6m)	6 yards (5.5m)

Cutting All measurements include ¼" (0.5cm) seam allowances.

	Lap	Twin XL	Queen
From the background fabric, cut	3 strips, 21" x 42" (53.3 x 106.7cm) 2 strips, 9" x 42" (22.9 x 106.7cm), subcut 3 rectangles, 9" x 21" (22.9 x 53.3cm) 4 strips, 6" x 42" (15.2 x 106.7cm)	4 strips, 21" x 42" (53.3 x 106.7cm) 2 strips, 18" x 42" (45.7 x 106.7cm), subcut 4 rectangles, 18" x 21" (45.7 x 53.3cm) 4 strips, 13½" x 42" (34.3 x 106.7cm)	2 strips, 72" x 42" (182.9 x 106.7cm), subcut crosswise 4 strips, 21" x 72" (53.3 x 182.9cm) 5 strips, 13½" x 42" (34.3 x 106.7cm)

Note: Seam allowances should be pressed after each join. Press open or press alternating rows/columns toward the darker fabric based on your preference.

For the corresponding quilt top, Spooky Spiderweb, see page 146.

The Log Cabin is made by "circling" strips around a center block. This design for the quilt back makes a fun match with the octagons on the front.

MAKE THE BLOCKS

1. Lay out one scrap square of any size for the center unit of the log cabin block, OR sew two short scrap rectangles together to make the center unit as shown. Note that the center unit does not need to be perfectly square for this block. It can be rectangular, but should be close to a square shape.

2. Lay out a scrap rectangle on the side of the center unit. The scrap rectangle should be the same length or longer than the center unit. Sew the rectangle to the side of the center unit and trim away any excess length as shown.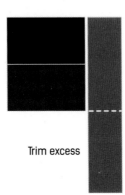

Trim excess

3. Rotate the block so the scrap rectangle sewn in step 2 is at the top. Then repeat this process, sewing a second scrap rectangle to the side of the unit, and trimming away any excess length from the scrap rectangle.

> Using strips of various width in the log cabin block gives it a fun, funky look.

4. Repeat this process, sewing scrap rectangles around the center unit until the log cabin block measures approximately 21" (53.3cm) square. Trim the block to 21" (53.3cm) long if necessary. The block must measure 21" long, but may be slightly wider for a rectangular log cabin block.

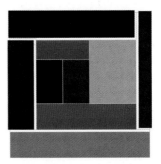

Make three total blocks for the Lap size, or four total blocks for the Twin XL and Queen sizes.

> If needed, use a little extra background fabric to widen your blocks to the correct size.

ASSEMBLE THE QUILT BACK

5. For the Lap size, sew one 9" x 21" (22.9 x 53.3cm) background rectangle to the end of one 21" x 42" (53.3 x 106.7cm) background rectangle to make one long strip, 21" x 51" (53.3 x 129.6cm). Make three total long strips.

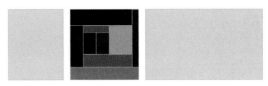

6. Cut one long background strip crosswise in a random place to make two lengths, each 21" (53.3cm) wide. Sew a log cabin block between the two lengths as shown. Repeat this process to make three rows. Note that the random cuts should be in different places for each long strip.

7. Refer to the Lap Quilt Assembly Diagram to lay out the three rows and sew them together as shown. Then, sew two 6" x 42" (15.2 x 106.7cm) background strips together, end to end, to make one long strip, measuring 6" x 84" (15.2 x 213.4cm), and sew the strip to the top of the backing. Trim away the excess length, and then repeat this process on the bottom as shown to complete the quilt back.

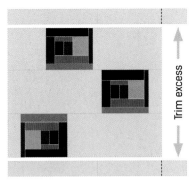

8. For the Twin XL size, sew an 18" x 21" (45.7 x 53.3cm) background rectangle to the end of one 21" x 42" (53.3 x 106.7cm) background strip to make one long strip, measuring 21" x 60" (53.3 x 152.4cm). Make four long strips.

9. Cut one long background strip crosswise in a random place to make two lengths, each 21" (53.3cm) wide. Sew a log cabin block between the two lengths as shown in step 6. Repeat this process to make four rows. Note that the random cuts should be in different places for each long strip.

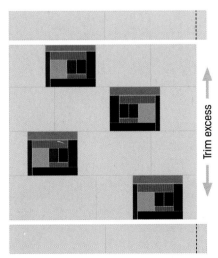

10. Refer to the Twin XL Quilt Assembly Diagram to lay out the four rows and sew them together as shown. Then, sew two 13½" x 42" (34.5 x 106.7cm) background strips together, end to end, to make one long strip, measuring 13½" x 84" (34.5 x 213.4cm). Sew the strip to the top of the rows and trim away the excess length. Repeat this process on the bottom as shown to complete the quilt back.

11. For the Queen size, cut one 21" x 72" (53.3 x 182.9cm) background strip crosswise in a random place to make two lengths, each 21" (53.3cm) wide, and sew a log cabin block between the two lengths as shown in step 6. Repeat this process to make four rows. Note that the random cuts should be in different places for each long strip.

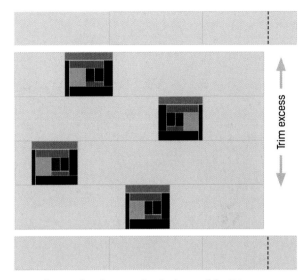

12. Refer to the Queen Quilt Assembly Diagram to lay out the four rows and sew them together as shown. Then, sew three 13½" x 42" (34.3 x 106.7cm) background strips together, end to end, to make one long strip, measuring 13½" x 126" (34.3 x 320cm). Sew the strip to the top of the rows and trim away the excess length. Then repeat this process on the bottom as shown to complete the quilt back.

FINISH THE QUILT

Refer to the Basting and Quilt Finishing section on page 138 for instructions on basting, quilting, and binding your quilt.

13. Layer the backing, batting, and quilt top and baste the layers together. Hand- or machine-quilt as desired.

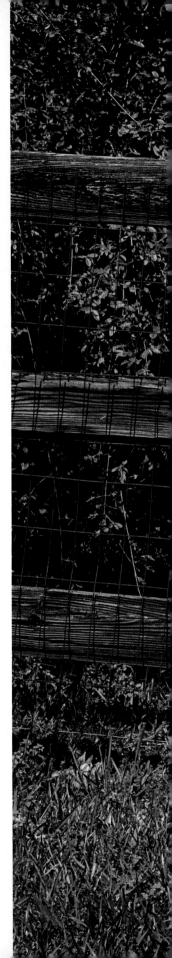

PART 3

Stash and Yardage Backs

If your quilt pattern doesn't afford any leftovers at all, or if you simply want to make a backing with yardage instead, go for it! These quilt backs may use a limited number of fabrics, but they're anything but drab! Just a few coordinating fabrics and some easy cutting and piecing, you can put together a show-stopping quilt back in no time.

The jumbo block in the Great Big Granny quilt back (page 122) makes quite a statement.

Checkerboard

....

SKILL LEVEL ✳ ✳ ✳ ✳ ✳
Beginner

If you need a little extra length or width for any size, just add an extra row of squares and adjust the fabric requirements accordingly. It's so easy!

A checkerboard design is a simple classic, yet so satisfying. It can be traditional, modern, minimal, or bold—all depending on the fabrics you choose. Alternating just two fabrics makes quite an impact on this backing.

FINISHED BACKING DIMENSIONS

Lap 62" x 82" (157.5 x 208.3cm)

Twin XL 82" x 103" (208.3 x 261.6cm)

Queen 103" x 103" (261.6 x 261.6cm)

Materials Yardage is based on 42" (106.7cm) wide fabric.

	Lap	Twin XL	Queen
Print A (coral)	1¾ yards (1.6m)	3 yards (2.7m)	4⅛ yards (3.8m)
Print B (teal)	1¾ yards (1.6m)	3 yards (2.7m)	3½ yards (3.2m)

Cutting All measurements include ¼" (0.5cm) seam allowances.

	Lap	Twin XL	Queen
From print A (coral), cut	3 strips, 21" x 42" (53.3 x 106.7cm), subcut 6 squares, 21" (53.3cm)	5 strips, 21" x 42" (53.3 x 106.7cm), subcut 10 squares, 21" (53.3cm)	7 strips, 21" x 42" (53.3 x 106.7cm), subcut 13 squares, 21" (53.3cm) (yields 1 extra)
From print B (teal), cut	3 strips, 21" x 42" (53.3 x 106.7cm), subcut 6 squares, 21" (53.3cm)	5 strips, 21" x 42" (53.3 x 106.7cm), subcut 10 squares, 21" (53.3cm)	6 strips, 21" x 42" (53.3 x 106.7cm), subcut 12 squares, 21" (53.3cm)

Note: Seam allowances should be pressed after each join. Press open or press alternating rows/columns toward the darker fabric based on your preference.

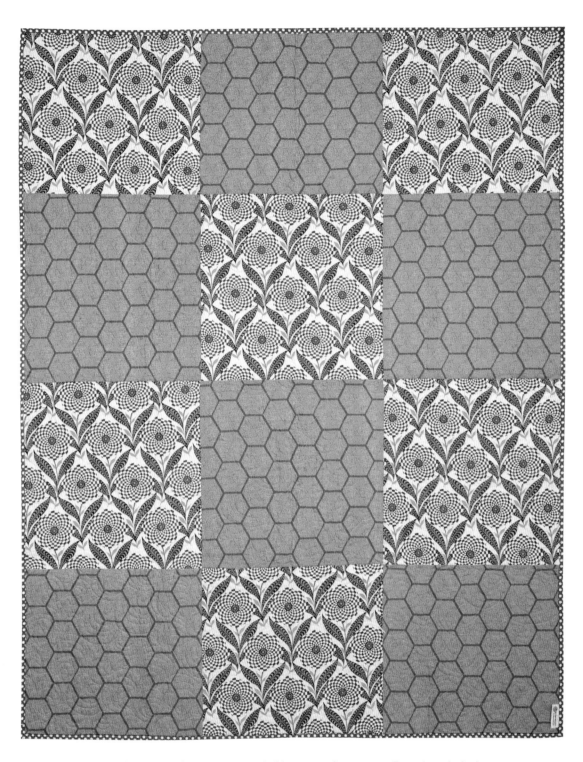

Because this design uses large squares, a bold print can't go amiss. Even though the hexagons and geometric flowers are both larger prints, they play so well together!

ASSEMBLE THE QUILT BACK

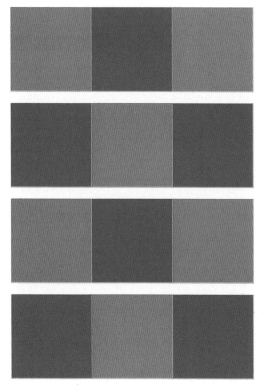

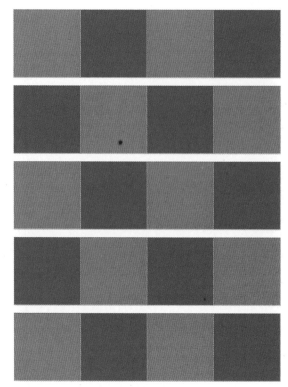

1. For the Lap size, refer to the Lap Quilt Assembly Diagram to lay out the print A and B squares into four rows with three squares in each row, alternating the colors as shown. Sew the rows together to complete the quilt backing.

2. For the Twin XL size, refer to the Twin XL Quilt Assembly Diagram to lay out the print A and B squares into five rows with four squares in each row, alternating the colors as shown. Sew the rows together to complete the quilt backing.

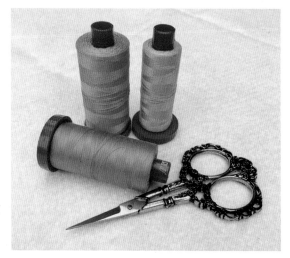

Not sure what color thread to use for quilting? Let your quilt back be your guide! Matching your thread to your quilt back creates a fun effect.

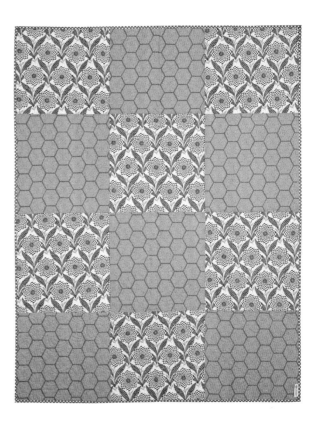

FINISH THE QUILT

Refer to the Basting and Quilt Finishing section on page 138 for instructions on basting, quilting, and binding your quilt.

4. Layer the backing, batting, and quilt top and baste the layers together. Hand- or machine-quilt as desired.

3. For the Queen size, refer to the Queen Quilt Assembly Diagram to lay out the print A and B squares into five rows with five squares in each row, alternating the colors as shown. Sew the rows together to complete the quilt backing.

The Checkerboard quilt back is another great choice for large-scale prints. Let those fabrics shine by leaving them in large chunks.

Walking Path

SKILL LEVEL ✳ ✳ ✳ ✳ ✳
Beginner

Do you have a gorgeous fabric that you want to show off? A Walking Path backing is the perfect place. With just two vertical seams, this quilt back is practically as easy as a single fabric backing, but the contrast stripe makes it so much more interesting.

FINISHED BACKING DIMENSIONS

Lap 72" x 72" (182.9 x 182.9cm)

Twin XL 77" x 108" (195.6 x 274.3cm)

Queen 90" x 108" (228.6 x 274.3cm)

Materials Yardage is based on 42" (106.7cm) wide fabric.

	Lap	Twin XL	Queen
Print A (main fabric)	3 yards (2.7m)	4½ yards (4.1m)	5 yards (4.6m)
Print B (contrast stripe)	⅔ yards (61.3cm)	1½ yards (1.4m)	2 yards (1.8m)

Cutting All measurements include ¼" (0.5cm) seam allowances.

	Lap	Twin XL	Queen
From print A (main fabric), cut	2 strips, 18" x 42" (45.7 x 106.7cm) *The remaining piece of fabric should measure 2 yards, 72" x 42" (182.9 x 106.7cm) after the selvages are removed	3 strips, 18" x 42" (45.7 x 106.7cm) *The remaining piece of fabric should measure 3 yards, 108" x 42" (274.3 x 106.7cm) after the selvages are removed	3 strips, 24" x 42" (61 x 106.7cm) *The remaining piece of fabric should measure 3 yards, 108" x 42" (274.3 x 106.7cm) after the selvages are removed
From print B (contrast stripe), cut	2 strips, 12" x 42" (30.5 x 106.7cm)	3 strips, 18" x 42" (45.7 x 106.7cm)	3 strips, 24" x 42" (61 x 106.7cm)

Note: Seam allowances should be pressed after each join. Press open or press alternating rows/columns toward the darker fabric based on your preference.

For the corresponding quilt top, Chapel Glass, see page 146.

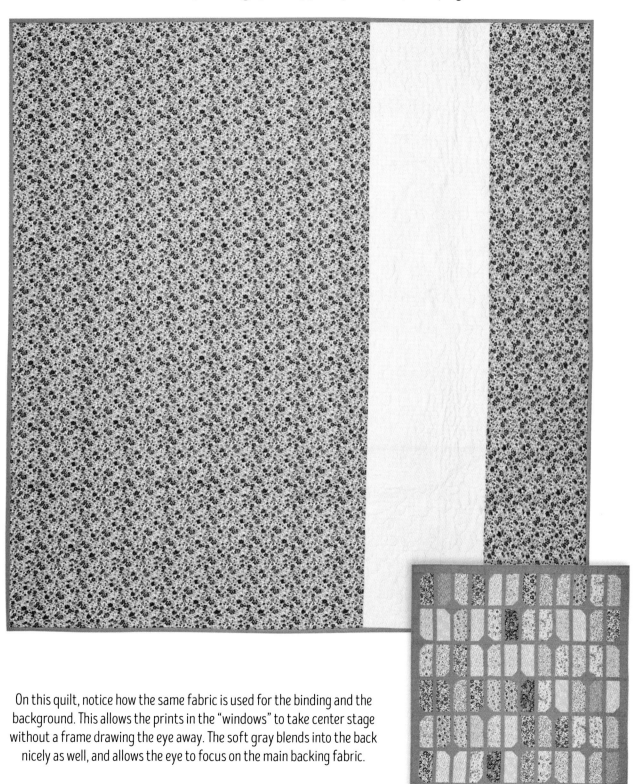

On this quilt, notice how the same fabric is used for the binding and the background. This allows the prints in the "windows" to take center stage without a frame drawing the eye away. The soft gray blends into the back nicely as well, and allows the eye to focus on the main backing fabric.

ASSEMBLE THE QUILT BACK

1. For the lap size, sew the two 18" x 42" (45.7 x 106.7cm) strips of print A to make one long strip measuring 18" x 84" (45.7 x 213.4cm). Repeat this process, sewing the two 12" x 42" (30.5 x 106.7cm) strips of print B to make one long strip.

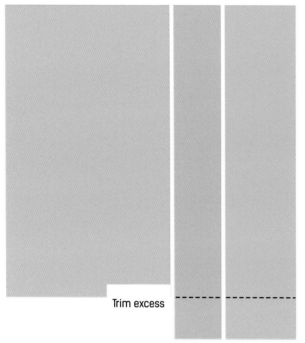

Trim excess

Trim excess

2. Refer to the Lap Quilt Assembly Diagram to lay out the two sewn strips and the 42" x 72" (106.7 x 182.9cm) piece of print A into three columns as shown. Sew the columns together and trim the excess length from the sewn strips to complete the backing.

3. For the Twin XL size, use the same process to sew the three 18" x 42" (45.7 x 106.7cm) print A strips into one long strip measuring 18" x 126" (45.7 x 320cm). Then sew the three print B strips into one long strip measuring 18" x 126" (45.7 x 320cm). Refer to the Twin XL Quilt Assembly Diagram to lay out the sewn strips and the 42" x 108" (106.7 x 274.3cm) piece of print A into three columns. Sew the three columns together and trim the excess length from the sewn strips to complete the backing.

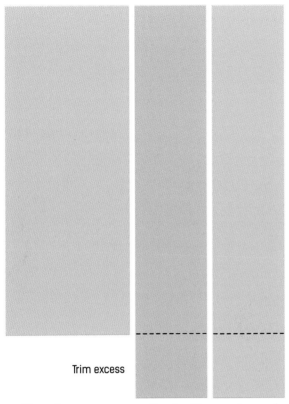

Trim excess

4. Follow the same process for the Queen size and sew the three 24" x 42" (61 x 106.7cm) print A strips into one long strip measuring 24" x 126" (61 x 320cm). Then sew the three print B strips into one long strip measuring 24" x 126" (61 x 320cm). Refer to the Queen Quilt Assembly Diagram to lay out the sewn strips and the 42" x 108" (106.7 x 274.3cm) piece of print A into three columns. Sew the three columns together and trim the excess length from the sewn strips to complete the backing.

FINISH THE QUILT

Refer to the Basting and Quilt Finishing section on page 138 for instructions on basting, quilting, and binding your quilt.

5. Layer the backing, batting, and quilt top and baste the layers together. Hand- or machine-quilt as desired.

The simplicity of this design leaves a lot of room for creativity. Contrasting prints, minimalistic solids, or even an embroidered feature would all work here.

Islands

SKILL LEVEL ✳ ✳ ✳ ✳ ✳
Confident Beginner

There are some really beautiful large-print fabrics out there in the world, and though it can sometimes be difficult to fit them into a quilt top, the back is always a wonderful place to show them off. The Islands backing uses just a bit of focus fabric, but the unexpected layout makes it the star.

FINISHED BACKING DIMENSIONS

Lap 72" x 76" (182.9 x 193cm)

Twin XL 80" x 108" (203.2 x 274.3cm)

Queen 100" x 108" (254 x 274.3cm)

Materials Yardage is based on 42" (106.7cm) wide fabric.

	Lap	Twin XL	Queen
Focus Fabric (Islands)	1⅛ yard (1m)	1¾ yard (1.6m)	2⅓ yard (2.1m)
Non-directional Background fabric	3⅛ yards (2.9m)	4⅔ yards (4.3m)	5¾ yards (5.3m)

Cutting All measurements include ¼" (0.5cm) seam allowances.

	Lap	Twin XL	Queen
From the Focus Fabric (Islands), cut	1 strip, 18½" x 42" (47 x 106.7cm), subcut 1 rectangle, 18½" x 19½" (47 x 49.5cm) 1 rectangle, 10½" x 18½" (26.7 x 47cm) 1 rectangle, 8½" x 18½" (21.6 x 47cm) 1 strip, 18½" x 42" (47 x 106.7cm), subcut 1 rectangle, 13½" x 18½" (34.3 x 47cm) 1 rectangle, 16½" x 18½" (41.9 x 47cm)	1 strip, 20½" x 42" (52.1 x 106.7cm), subcut 1 rectangle, 20½" x 24½" (52.1 x 62.2cm) 1 rectangle, 16½" x 20½" (41.9 x 52.1cm) 1 strip, 20½" x 42" (52.1 x 106.7cm), subcut 1 rectangle, 18½" x 20½" (47 x 52.1cm) 1 rectangle, 12½" x 20½" (31.8 x 52.1cm) 1 rectangle, 8½" x 20½" (21.6 x 52.1cm) 1 strip, 20½" x 42" (52.1 x 106.7cm), subcut 1 rectangle, 12½" x 20½" (31.8 x 52.1cm) 1 rectangle, 6½" x 20½" (16.5 x 52.1cm)	1 strip, 20½" x 42" (52.1 x 106.7cm), subcut 1 rectangle, 20½" x 24½" (52.1 x 62.2cm) 1 rectangle, 16½" x 20½" (41.9 x 52.1cm) 1 strip, 20½" x 42" (52.1 x 106.7cm), subcut 1 rectangle, 18½" x 20½" (47 x 52.1cm) 1 rectangle, 12½" x 20½" (31.8 x 52.1cm) 1 rectangle, 8½" x 20½" (21.6 x 52.1cm) 1 strip, 20½" x 42" (52.1 x 106.7cm), subcut 1 rectangle, 12½" x 20½" (31.8 x 52.1cm) 1 rectangle, 6½" x 20½" (16.5 x 52.1cm) 1 strip, 20½" x 42" (52.1 x 106.7cm), subcut 2 rectangles, 12½" x 20½" (31.8 x 52.1cm)
From the background fabric, cut	6 strips, 18½" x 42" (47 x 106.7cm) From 2 strips, subcut 4 rectangles, 18½" x 21" (47 x 53.3cm)	8 strips, 20½" x 42" (52.1 x 106.7cm)	10 strips, 20½" x 42" (52.1 x 106.7cm)

Note: Seam allowances should be pressed after each join. Press open or press alternating rows/columns toward the darker fabric based on your preference.

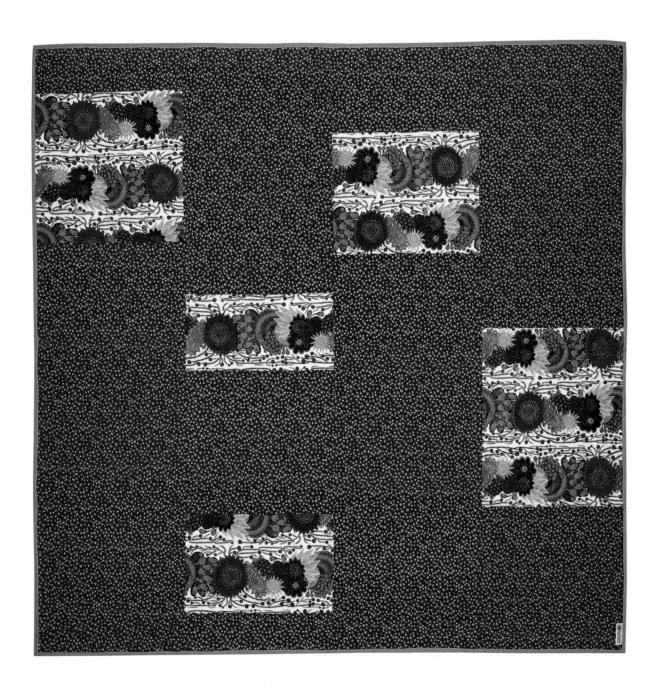

You don't have to choose a solid fabric for the background of this quilt back. This small print coordinates with the Island fabric beautifully, and the overall effect is not too busy!

ASSEMBLE THE QUILT BACK

1. For the Lap size, sew one 18½" x 42" (47 x 106.7cm) background strip and one 18½" x 21" (47 x 53.3cm) background rectangle together to make one long strip, 18½" x 63" (47 x 160cm). Make four long strips.

Trim excess

2. Refer to the Lap Quilt Assembly Diagram to cut one long strip crosswise in a random place, and sew the 18½" x 19½" (47 x 49.5cm) rectangle "island" between the two pieces to make column 1. Repeat this process for columns 2–4, using the notes that follow.

To ensure your islands are "floating" where you want them, lay out each column individually before cutting the strips.

I featured one large print in this quilt back, but you could use a different print for each island. Or flip the design and use a large print in the background with floating solid rectangles!

- **Column 2:** Cut the strip and sew the 13½" x 18½" (34.3 x 47cm) island between the cut pieces.

- **Column 3:** Cut the strip *in two places* and sew the 10½" x 18½" (26.7 x 47cm) island, plus the 8½" x 18½" (21.6 x 47cm) island between the cut pieces.

- **Column 4:** Cut the strip and sew the 16½" x 18½" (41.9 x 47cm) island between the cut pieces.

3. Sew the columns together, and then trim the columns to 76" (193cm) long (the length of column 2) to complete the quilt back.

4. For the Twin XL size, sew two 20½" x 42" (52.1 x 106.7cm) background strips together to make one long strip, 20½" x 84" (52.1 x 213.4cm). Make four long strips.

5. Refer to the Twin XL Quilt Assembly Diagram to cut one long strip crosswise in two random places, and sew the 18½" x 20½" (47 x 52.1cm) rectangle "island", plus the 6½" x 20½" (16.5 x 52.1cm) island between the cut pieces to make column 1. Repeat this process for columns 2–4. Each column should measure 20½" x 108" (52.1 x 274.3cm). Then sew the four columns together to complete the quilt back.

- **Column 2:** Cut the strip and sew the 20½" x 24½" (52.1 x 62.2cm) island between the cut pieces.

- **Column 3:** Cut the strip *in two places* and sew two 12½" x 20½" (31.8 x 52.1cm) islands between the cut pieces.

- **Column 4:** Cut the strip *in two places* and sew the 8½" x 20½" (21.6 x 52.1cm) island, plus the 16½" x 20½" (41.9 x 52.1cm) island between the cut pieces.

6. For the Queen size, follow the same process in step 4 to make *five* long strips, and then follow step 5 to complete columns 1-4. Next, refer to the Queen Quilt Assembly Diagram to cut the fifth long strip in two random places and sew two 12½" x 20½" (31.8 x 52.1cm) islands between the cut pieces to complete the final column. Each column should measure 20½" x 108" (52.1 x 274.3cm). Sew the five columns together to complete the quilt back.

FINISH THE QUILT

Refer to the Basting and Quilt Finishing section on page 138 for instructions on basting, quilting, and binding your quilt.

7. Layer the backing, batting, and quilt top and baste the layers together. Hand- or machine-quilt as desired.

Broken Rugby Stripe

SKILL LEVEL ✳ ✳ ✳ ✳ ✳
Confident Beginner

Whether you're working with solids or prints, bold stripes are a simple way to make the backing of your quilt pop. Just choose three coordinating fabrics and let these stripes bring the "wow factor."

FINISHED BACKING DIMENSIONS

Lap 72" x 73" (182.9 x 185.4cm)

Twin XL 84" x 105" (213.4 x 266.7cm)

Queen 93" x 105" (236.2 x 266.7cm)

Materials Yardage is based on 42" (106.7cm) wide fabric.

	Lap	Twin XL	Queen
Print A (light blue)	1¾ yards (1.6m)	3⅛ yards (2.9m)	3¼ yards (3m)
Print B (navy)	1⅓ yards (1.2m)	2⅔ yards (2.4m)	2⅞ yards (2.6m)
Print C (berry)	1 yard (91.4cm)	1½ yards (1.4m)	2 yards (1.8m)

Cutting All measurements include ¼" (0.5cm) seam allowances.

	Lap	Twin XL	Queen
From print A (light blue), cut	4 strips, 15½" x 42" (39.4 x 106.7cm), subcut from 1 strip, 3 rectangles, 12½" x 15½" (31.8 x 39.4cm)	4 strips, 15½" x 42" (39.4 x 106.7cm) 2 strips, 24½" x 42" (62.2 x 106.7cm), subcut 4 rectangles, 15½" x 24½" (39.4 x 62.2cm)	4 strips, 15½" x 42" (39.4 x 106.7cm) 2 strips, 27½" x 42" (69.9 x 106.7cm), subcut 4 rectangles, 15½" x 27½" (39.4 x 69.9cm)
From print B (navy), cut	3 strips, 15½" x 42" (39.4 x 106.7cm), subcut from 1 strip, 2 rectangles, 12½" x 15½" (31.8 x 39.4cm)	3 strips, 15½" x 42" (39.4 x 106.7cm) 2 strips, 24½" x 42" (62.2 x 106.7cm), subcut 3 rectangles, 15½" x 24½" (39.4 x 62.2cm)	3 strips, 15½" x 42" (39.4 x 106.7cm) 2 strips, 27½" x 42" (69.9 x 106.7cm), subcut 3 rectangles, 15½" x 27½" (39.4 x 69.9cm)
From print C (berry), cut	2 strips, 18" x 42" (45.7 x 106.7cm)	3 strips, 18" x 42" (45.7 x 106.7cm)	3 strips, 24" x 42" (61 x 106.7cm)

Note: Seam allowances should be pressed after each join. Press open or press alternating rows/columns toward the darker fabric based on your preference.

For the corresponding quilt top, Marquise, see page 146.

I love using prints, but solid colors can make a huge impact. These high-contrast, solid colors allow the pattern to make a graphic statement.

ASSEMBLE THE QUILT BACK

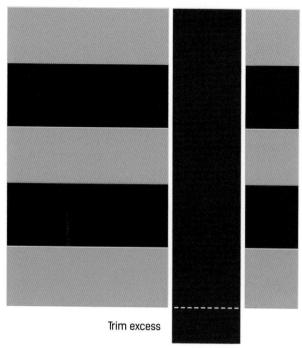

Trim excess

1. For the Lap size, refer to the Lap Quilt Assembly Diagram to lay out the long print A and print B rectangles, alternating the colors as shown. Sew the long rectangles together to make one column measuring 42" x 75" (106.7 x 190.5cm).

2. Lay out the short print A and print B rectangles, alternating the colors as shown in the Lap Quilt Assembly Diagram, using the same color layout as step 1. Sew the short rectangles together to make one column measuring 12½" x 75" (31.8 x 190.5cm).

3. Sew the two print C rectangles end-to-end to yield one long strip measuring 18" x 84" (45.7 x 213.4cm).

4. Refer to the Lap Quilt Assembly Diagram to lay out all three columns, and sew the columns together as shown. Trim the excess length from the print C strip to complete the backing.

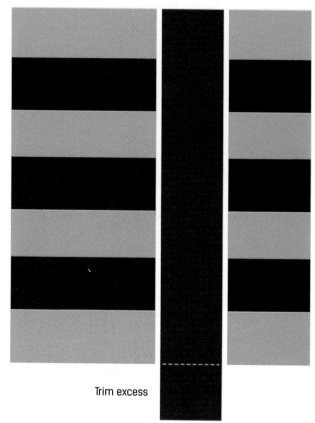

Trim excess

5. For the Twin XL size, use the same process. Refer to the Twin XL Quilt Assembly Diagram to sew the long print A and B rectangles, and short print A and B rectangles into columns as shown. Then, sew the three print C rectangles end-to-end to yield one long strip measuring 18" x 126" (45.7 x 320cm). Sew the Twin XL backing in three columns, and trim the excess length from the print C strip to complete the backing.

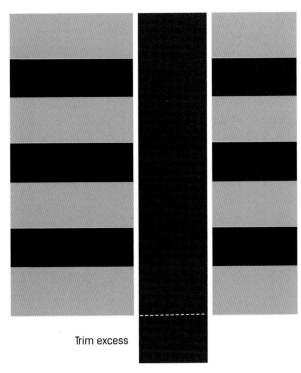

Trim excess

FINISH THE QUILT

Refer to the Basting and Quilt Finishing section on page 138 for instructions on basting, quilting, and binding your quilt.

7. Layer the backing, batting, and quilt top and baste the layers together. Hand- or machine-quilt as desired.

6. For the Queen size, use the same process. Refer to the Queen Quilt Assembly Diagram to sew the long print A and B rectangles, and short print A and B rectangles into columns as shown. Then, sew the three print C rectangles end-to-end to yield one long strip measuring 24" x 126" (61 x 320cm). Sew the Queen backing in three columns and trim the excess length from the print C strip to complete the backing.

Of course this backing would look great with three contrasting prints, but even if your quilt is made from prints, consider a backing made from coordinating solids!

Tunnel Vision

SKILL LEVEL ✳ ✳ ✳ ✳ ✳
Confident Beginner

With just one main fabric and an accent fabric, the Tunnel Vision back is so easy to put together, but the way these fabrics are arranged gives it lots of interest.

FINISHED BACKING DIMENSIONS

Lap 69" x 74" (175.3 x 188cm)

Twin XL 84" x 105" (213.4 x 266.7cm)

Queen 96" x 108" (243.8 x 274.3cm)

Materials Yardage is based on 42" (106.7cm) wide fabric.

	Lap	Twin XL	Queen
Main fabric (navy)	3 yards (2.7m)	4½ yards (4.1m)	5⅓ yards (4.9m)
Accent fabric (red)	⅞ yard (80cm)	1⅔ yards (1.5m)	2⅓ yards (2.1m)

Cutting All measurements include ¼" (0.5cm) seam allowances.

	Lap	Twin XL	Queen
From the main fabric (navy), cut	3 strips, 18½" x 42" (47 x 106.7cm), subcut from 1 strip, 1 rectangle, 9½" x 18½" (24.1 x 47cm) Leave the remaining 1⅓ yard (1.2m) uncut.	4 strips, 24½" x 42" (62.2 x 106.7cm), subcut from 1 strip, 1 rectangle, 18½" x 24½" (47 x 62.2cm) 1 rectangle 21½" x 24½" (54.6 x 62.2cm) Leave the remaining 1¾ yard (1.6m) uncut.	5 strips, 27½" x 42" (69.9 x 106.7cm), subcut from 1 strip, 1 square, 27½" (69.9cm) subcut from 1 strip, 1 rectangle 24½" x 27½" (62.2 x 69.9cm) Leave the remaining 1½ yard (1.4m) uncut.
From the accent fabric (red), cut	3 strips, 9½" x 42" (24.1 x 106.7cm)	3 strips, 18½" x 42" (47 x 106.7cm)	3 strips, 27½" x 42" (69.9 x 106.7cm)

Note: Seam allowances should be pressed after each join. Press open or press alternating rows/columns toward the darker fabric based on your preference.

Instead of using a print accent fabric, think of your main fabric as a feature,
and use a solid or small print to "frame it"!

ASSEMBLE THE QUILT BACK

1. For the Lap size, refer to the Lap Quilt Assembly Diagram to lay out the 1⅓ yard (1.2m) piece of the main fabric, and sew one 9½" x 42" (24.1 x 106.7cm) strip of accent fabric to the top of the piece as shown. Then, sew two 9½" x 42" (24.1 x 106.7cm) strips of accent fabric together to make one long strip, 9½" x 84" (24.1 x 213.4cm). Sew it to the side of the backing. Trim away the excess length from the accent fabric strip.

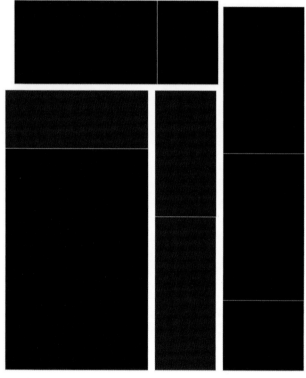

2. Then, sew one 18½" x 42" (47 x 106.7cm) strip and the 9½" x 18½" (24.1 x 47cm) rectangle of the main fabric together to make a long strip measuring 18½" x 51" (47 x 129.5cm). Sew it to the top of the unit from step 1. Sew the two remaining 18½" (47cm) strips of main fabric together to make one long strip. Sew it to the side of the backing as shown to complete the quilt back.

3. For the Twin XL size, refer to the Twin XL Quilt Assembly Diagram to lay out the 1¾-yard (1.6m) piece of the main fabric, and sew one 18½" x 42" (47 x 106.7cm) strip of accent fabric to the top of the piece as shown. Then, sew two 18½" x 42" (47 x 106.7cm) strips of accent fabric together to make one long strip, 18½" x 84" (47 x 213.4cm). Sew it to the side of the backing. Trim away the excess length from the accent fabric strip.

4. Then, sew one 24½" x 42" (62.2 x 106.7cm) strip and the 18½" x 24½" (47 x 62.2cm) rectangle of the main fabric together to make a long strip measuring 24½" x 60" (62.2 x 152.4cm). Sew it to the top of the unit from step 3. Sew two 24½" x 42" (62.2 x 106.7cm) strips and one 21½" x 24½" (54.6 x 62.2cm) rectangle of the main fabric to make one long strip. Sew it to the side the backing as shown. Trim away the excess length from the long strip to complete the quilt back.

FINISH THE QUILT

5. For the Queen size, refer to the Queen Quilt Assembly Diagram to lay out the 1½-yard (1.6m) piece of the main fabric, and sew one 27½" x 42" (69.9 x 106.7cm) strip of accent fabric to the top of the piece as shown. Then, sew two 27½" x 42" (69.9 x 106.7cm) strips of accent fabric together to make one long strip, 27½" x 84" (69.9 x 213.4cm). Sew it to the side of the backing. Trim away the excess length from the accent fabric strip.

Refer to the Basting and Quilt Finishing section on page 138 for instructions on basting, quilting, and binding your quilt.

7. Layer the backing, batting, and quilt top and baste the layers together. Hand- or machine-quilt as desired.

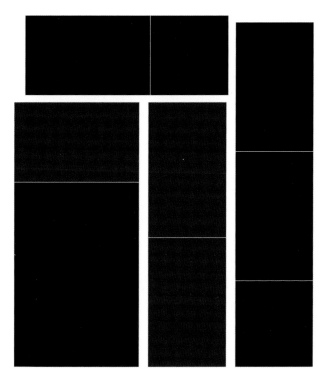

6. Then, sew one 27½" x 42" (69.9 x 106.7cm) strip and the 27½" (69.9cm) square of the main fabric together to make a long strip measuring 27½" x 69" (69.9 x 175.3cm). Sew it to the top of the unit from step 5. Sew two 27½" x 42" (69.9 x 106.7cm) strips, and one 24½" x 27½" (62.2 x 69.9cm) rectangle of main fabric to make one long strip. Sew it to the side of the backing as shown. Trim away the excess length from the long strip to complete the quilt back.

Focus Stripe

SKILL LEVEL ✳ ✳ ✳ ✳ ✳
Beginner

Similar to the Walking Path backing, with just one additional fabric, a Focus Stripe back is another fantastic place to show off a special fabric. In this design, the focus fabric is centered in the back, drawing the eye.

FINISHED BACKING DIMENSIONS

Lap 70" x 84" (177.8 x 213.4cm)

Twin XL 83" x 105" (210.8 x 266.7cm)

Queen 96" x 105" (243.8 x 266.7cm)

Materials Yardage is based on 42" (106.7cm) wide fabric.

	Lap	Twin XL	Queen
Print A (center stripe)	1 yard (91.4cm)	2 yards (1.8m)	2 yards (1.8m)
Print B (middle stripes)	1½ yards (1.4m)	2¼ yards (2.1m)	2⅔ yards (2.4m)
Print C (edge stripes)	1½ yards (1.4m)	2¼ yards (2.1m)	2⅔ yards (2.4m)

Cutting All measurements include ¼" (0.5cm) seam allowances.

	Lap	Twin XL	Queen
From print A (center stripe), cut	2 strips, 18" x 42" (45.7 x 106.7cm)	3 strips, 24" x 42" (61 x 106.7cm), subcut from one strip, 1 rectangle, 21" x 24" (53.3 x 61cm)	3 strips, 24" x 42" (61 x 106.7cm), subcut from one strip, 1 rectangle, 21" x 24" (53.3 x 61cm)
From prints B and C (middle stripes), cut from each	4 strips, 13½" x 42" (34.3 x 106.7cm)	5 strips, 15½" x 42" (39.4 x 106.7cm) subcut from one strip, 2 rectangles 15½" x 21" (39.4 x 61cm)	5 strips, 18½" x 42" (47 x 106.7cm), subcut from one strip, 2 rectangles 18½" x 21" (47 x 53.3cm)

Note: Seam allowances should be pressed after each join. Press open or press alternating rows/columns toward the darker fabric based on your preference.

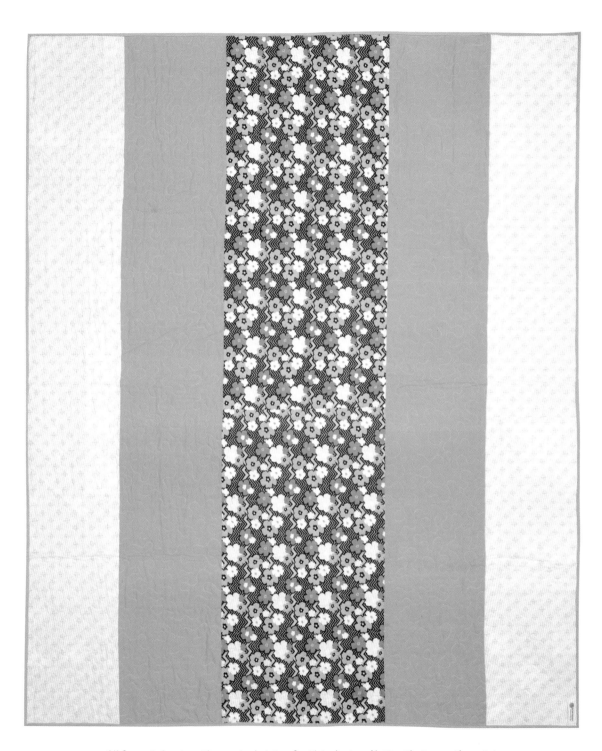

All focus is kept on the central stripe for this design. Notice that even the print used for the far left and right sides is soft and unobtrusive.

ASSEMBLE THE QUILT BACK

1. For the Lap size, sew the two 18" x 42" (45.7 x 106.7cm) strips of print A to make one long strip measuring 18" x 84" (45.7 x 213.4cm) for the center of the backing.

2. Repeat this process to make two 13½" x 84" (34.3 x 213.4cm) strips of print B and two 13½" x 84" (34.3 x 213.4cm) strips of print C.

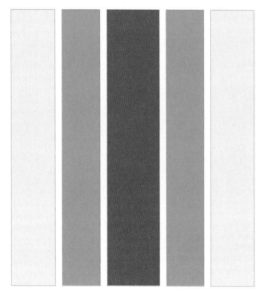

3. Refer to the Lap Quilt Assembly Diagram to lay out the five long strips into columns as shown and sew the columns together to complete the quilt back.

4. For the Twin XL size, use the same process to sew two 24" x 42" (61 x 106.7cm) strips of print A, plus one 21" x 24" (53.3 x 61cm) rectangle of print A into one long strip measuring 24" x 105" (61 x 266.7cm) for the center of the quilt. Then sew two print B strips, plus one 15½" x 21" (39.4 x 53.3cm) rectangle of print B into one long strip measuring 15½" x 105" (39.4 x 266.7cm). Make two long print B strips, and then use the same process to make two long print C strips, 15½" x 105" (39.4 x 266.7cm).

5. Refer to the Twin XL Quilt Assembly Diagram to lay out the five long strips into columns as shown and sew the columns together to complete the quilt back.

6. For the Queen size, use the same process to sew two 24" x 42" (61 x 106.7cm) strips of print A, plus one 21" x 24" (53.3 x 61cm) rectangle of print A into one long strip measuring 24" x 105" (61 x 266.7cm) for the center of the quilt. Then sew two print B strips, plus one 18½ x 21" (47 x 53.3cm) rectangle of print B into one long strip measuring 18½" x 105" (47 x 266.7cm). Make two long print B strips, and then use the same process to make two long print C strips, 18½" x 105" (47 x 266.7cm).

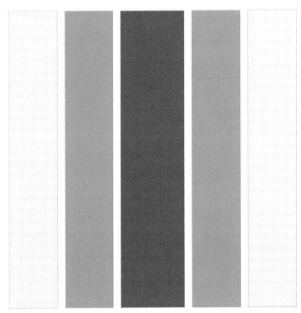

7. Refer to the Queen Quilt Assembly Diagram to lay out the five long strips into columns as shown and sew the columns together to complete the quilt back.

FINISH THE QUILT

Refer to the Basting and Quilt Finishing section on page 138 for instructions on basting, quilting, and binding your quilt.

8. Layer the backing, batting, and quilt top and baste the layers together. Hand- or machine-quilt as desired.

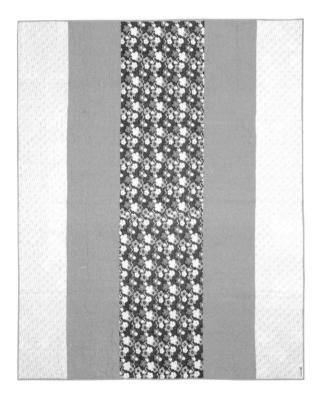

Don't Box Me In

SKILL LEVEL ✳ ✳ ✳ ✳ ✳
Confident Beginner

With giant squares and strips, this backing couldn't be quicker to put together, but rotating the units creates such a neat visual effect.

FINISHED BACKING DIMENSIONS

Lap 68" x 68" (172.7 x 172.7cm)

Twin XL 80" x 108" (203.2 x 274.3cm)

Queen 96" x 108" (243.8 x 274.3cm)

Materials Yardage is based on 42" (106.7cm) wide fabric.

	Lap	Twin XL	Queen
Print A (teal)	1⅛ yards (1m)	1¼ yards (1.1m)	1¼ yards (1.1m)
Print B (navy)	1¾ yards (1.6m)	3⅔ yards (3.4m)	4¼ yards (3.9m)
Print C (coral)	1¼ yards (1.1m)	1½ yards (1.4m)	1⅔ yards (1.5m)

Cutting All measurements include ¼" (0.5cm) seam allowances.

	Lap	Twin XL	Queen
From print A (teal), cut	2 strips, 18½" x 42" (47 x 106.7cm), subcut 4 squares, 18½" (47cm)	2 strips, 20½" x 42" (52.1 x 106.7cm), subcut 4 squares, 20½" (52.1cm)	2 strips, 20½" x 42" (52.1 x 106.7cm), subcut 4 squares, 20½" (52.1cm)
From print B (navy), cut	2 strips, 8½" x 42" (21.6 x 106.7cm), subcut 4 rectangles, 8½" x 18½" (21.6 x 47cm) 1 strip, 26½" x 42" (67.3 x 106.7cm), subcut 4 rectangles, 8½" x 26½" (21.6 x 67.3cm) 2 strips, 8½" x 42" (21.6 x 106.7cm), subcut 8 squares, 8½" (21.6cm)	1 strip, 20½" x 42" (52.1 x 106.7cm), subcut 4 rectangles, 10½" x 20½" (26.7 x 52.1cm) 1 strip, 30½" x 42" (77.5 x 106.7cm), subcut 4 rectangles, 10½" x 30½" (26.7 x 77.5cm) 2 strips, 10½" x 42" (26.7 x 106.7cm), subcut 8 squares, 10½" (26.7cm) 4 strips, 14½" x 42" (36.8 x 106.7cm)	2 strips, 14½" x 42" (36.8 x 106.7cm), subcut 4 rectangles, 14 ½" x 20½" (36.8 x 52.1cm) 2 strips, 14½" x 42" (36.8 x 106.7cm), subcut 4 rectangles, 14½" x 34½" (36.8 x 87.6cm) 4 strips, 14½" x 42" (36.8 x 106.7cm), subcut 8 squares, 14½" (36.8cm) 5 strips, 6½" x 42" (16.5 x 106.7cm), subcut from one strip, 2 rectangles, 6½" x 21" (16.5 x 53.3cm)
From print C (coral), cut	2 strips, 8½" x 42" (21.6 x 106.7cm), subcut 4 rectangles, 8½" x 18½" (21.6 x 47cm) 1 strip, 26½" x 42" (67.3 x 106.7cm), subcut 4 rectangles, 8½" x 26½" (21.6 x 67.3cm)	1 strip, 20½" x 42" (52.1 x 106.7cm), subcut 4 rectangles, 10½" x 20½" (26.7 x 52.1cm) 1 strip, 30½" x 42" (77.5 x 106.7cm), subcut 4 rectangles, 10½" x 30½" (26.7 x 77.5cm)	2 strips, 14½" x 42" (36.8 x 106.7cm), subcut 4 rectangles, 14½" x 20½" (36.8 x 52.1cm) 2 strips, 14½" x 42" (36.8 x 106.7cm), subcut 4 rectangles, 14½" x 34½" (36.8 x 87.6cm)

Note: Seam allowances should be pressed after each join. Press open or press alternating rows/columns toward the darker fabric based on your preference.

For the corresponding quilt top, French Tiles, see page 146.

The beauty of this quilt back design is that it looks complex, but it's really not! Clever fabric placement tricks the eye!

ASSEMBLE THE QUILT BACK

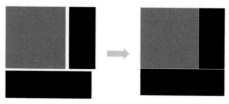

1. For the Lap size, sew an 8½" x 18½" (21.6 x 47cm) print B rectangle to the side of an 18½" (47cm) print A square. Then, sew an 8½" x 26½" (21.6 x 67.3cm) print B rectangle to the bottom of the unit as shown.

2. Sew one 8½" (21.6cm) print B square to the end of an 8½" x 18½" (21.6 x 47cm) print C rectangle. Then sew a second print B square to the end of an 8½" x 26½" (21.6 x 67.3cm) print C rectangle as shown.

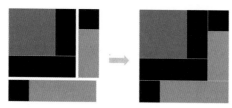

3. Sew the shorter print B/C strip to the side of the unit with the print B square pointed toward the top as shown. Then sew the longer B/C strip to the bottom of the unit with the print B square pointed toward the left to complete the unit. Make four total units for the Lap size.

4. Refer to the Lap Quilt Assembly Diagram to arrange the four units as shown, and sew the units together to complete the quilt back.

5a. Use the same process in steps 1–3 to make the units for the Twin XL size. Sew a 10½" x 20½" (26.7 x 52.1cm) print B rectangle to the side of a 20½" (52.1cm) print A square. Then, sew a 10½" x 30½" (26.7 x 77.5cm) print B rectangle to the bottom of the unit.

5b. Then sew one 10½" (26.7cm) print B square to the end of a 10½" x 20½" (26.7 x 52.1cm) print C rectangle. Sew a second print B square to the end of a 10½" x 30½" (26.7 x 77.5cm) print C rectangle as shown. Sew the shorter print B/C strip to the side of the unit with the print B square pointed toward the top as shown. Then sew the longer B/C strip to the bottom of the unit with the print B square pointed toward the left to complete the unit. Make four total units for the Twin XL size.

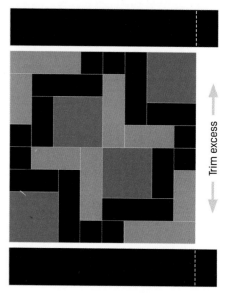

6. Sew two 14½" (36.8cm) print B strips end-to-end to make one long strip measuring 14½" x 84" (36.8 x 213.4cm). Make two total long strips. Refer to the Twin XL Quilt Assembly Diagram to arrange the four block units and sew them together as shown. Then sew the long strips to the top and bottom of the quilt. Trim the excess length from each long strip to complete the quilt back.

7a. Use the same process in steps 1–3 to make the units for the Queen size. Sew a 14½" x 20½" (36.8 x 52.1cm) print B rectangle to the side of a 20½" (52.1cm) print A square. Then, sew a 14½" x 34½" (36.8 x 87.6cm) print B rectangle to the bottom of the unit.

7b. Then sew one 14½" (36.8cm) print B square to the end of a 14½" x 20½" (36.8 x 52.1cm) print C rectangle. Sew a second print B square to the end of a 14½" x 34½" (36.8 x 87.6cm) print C rectangle as shown. Sew the shorter print B/C strip to the side of the unit with the print B square pointed toward the top as shown. Then sew the longer B/C strip to the bottom of the unit with the print B square pointed toward the left to complete the unit. Make four total units for the Queen size.

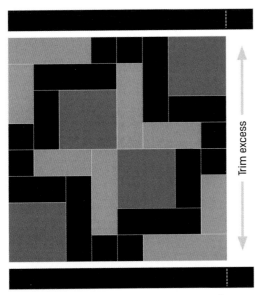

8. Sew two 6½" (16.5cm) print B strips, and one 6½" x 21" (16.5 x 53.3cm) print B rectangle end-to-end to make one long strip measuring 6½" x 104" (16.5 x 264.1cm). Make two total long strips. Refer to the Queen Quilt Assembly Diagram to arrange the four block units and sew them together as shown. Then sew the long strips to the top and bottom of the quilt. Trim the excess length from each long strip to complete the quilt back.

FINISH THE QUILT

Refer to the Basting and Quilt Finishing section on page 138 for instructions on basting, quilting, and binding your quilt.

9. Layer the backing, batting, and quilt top and baste the layers together. Hand- or machine-quilt as desired.

Don't Box Me In goes together quickly with just three fabrics.

Toppling Tower

SKILL LEVEL ✳ ✳ ✳ ✳ ✳
Confident Beginner

This fun backing looks like a stack of fabric getting ready to tumble down. Making fabric loops makes this quilt back a snap to put together.

FINISHED BACKING DIMENSIONS

Lap 72" x 72" (182.9 x 182.9cm)

Twin XL 84" x 108" (213.4 x 274.3cm)

Queen 96" x 108" (243.8 x 274.3cm)

Materials Yardage is based on 42" (106.7cm) wide fabric.

	Lap	Twin XL	Queen
Four coordinating fabric prints	⅔ yard (61cm) each	⅞ yard (80cm) each	⅞ yard (80cm) each
Background fabric	2¼ yards (2.1m)	3¼ yards (3m)	4¼ yards (3.9m)

Cutting All measurements include ¼" (0.5cm) seam allowances.

	Lap	Twin XL	Queen
From each print, cut	2 strips, 9½" x 42" (24.1 x 106.7cm)	3 strips, 9½" x 42" (24.1 x 106.7cm)	3 strips, 9½" x 42" (24.1 x 106.7cm)
From the background fabric, cut	8 strips, 9½" x 42" (24.1 x 106.7cm), subcut 8 rectangles, 9½" x 31" (24.1 x 78.7cm)	12 strips, 9½" x 42" (24.1 x 106.7cm)	16 strips, 9½" x 42" (24.1 x 106.7cm), subcut from four strips, 12 rectangles, 9½" x 12½" (24.1 x 31.8cm)

Note: Seam allowances should be pressed after each join. Press open or press alternating rows/columns toward the darker fabric based on your preference.

For the corresponding quilt top, MidMod Diamonds, see page 146.

The horizontal lines in the Toppling Tower design are a fun contrast to the vertical diamond blocks on the front of the quilt.

ASSEMBLE THE QUILT BACK

1. For the Lap size, sew a 9½" x 31" (24.1 x 78.7cm) background rectangle to *both ends* of a print strip to create a loop. Cut the background rectangle crosswise in a random place to make a row that measures 9½" x 72" (24.1 x 182.9cm).

2. Repeat this process using the remaining print strips and background rectangles to make eight total rows, two rows from each print. Lay out the rows, alternating the prints as shown, and sew the rows together to complete the quilt back.

Work from top to bottom, one loop at a time! Before making the random cut on each fabric loop, lay out the loop with the row above to make sure you're happy with the placement of the cut. Try to keep the quilt back balanced with an equal number of print strips to the left and right of center.

3. For the Twin XL size, use the same process in step 1 to sew a 9½" x 42" (24.1 x 106.7cm) print strip and a 9½" x 42" (24.1 x 106.7cm) background strip to make a fabric loop. Cut the background fabric crosswise in a random place to make a row measuring 9½" x 84" (24.1 x 213.4cm). Make twelve total rows for the Twin XL size, three rows for each print. Lay out the rows, alternating the prints as shown, and sew the rows together to complete the quilt back.

4. For the Queen size, sew one 9½" x 12½" (24.1 x 31.8cm) rectangle to one 9½" x 42" (24.1 x 106.7cm) strip to make one long background strip measuring 9½" x 54" (24.1 x 137.2cm). Make twelve total background strips.

FINISH THE QUILT

Refer to the Basting and Quilt Finishing section on page 138 for instructions on basting, quilting, and binding your quilt.

6. Layer the backing, batting, and quilt top and baste the layers together. Hand- or machine-quilt as desired.

The Toppling Tower quilt back gives lots of interest to simple strips.

5. Then, use the same process as step 1 to sew a 9½" x 42" (24.1 x 137.2cm) print strip and a 9½" x 54" (24.1 x 106.7cm) background strip to make a fabric loop. Cut the background fabric crosswise in a random place to make a row measuring 9½" x 96" (24.1 x 243.8cm). Make twelve total rows for the Queen size, three rows for each print. Lay out the rows, alternating the prints as shown, and sew the rows together to complete the quilt back.

Stash Rainbow

SKILL LEVEL ✳ ✳ ✳ ✳ ✳
Confident Beginner

There's something special about a rainbow. The way the colors gradually blend into one another is spectacular, and sometimes it's exactly what I want on the back of my quilt. A Stash Rainbow quilt back is another perfect one for shopping your fabric stash, and the results are sure to be fantastic.

FINISHED BACKING DIMENSIONS

Lap 84" x 84" (213.4 x 213.4cm)

Twin XL 84" x 126" (213.4 x 320cm)

Queen 100" x 126" (254 x 320cm)

Materials Yardage is based on 42" (106.7cm) wide fabric

The quilt back shown uses 12 fabrics. The exact number of fabrics required for your quilt back will be determined by the width of your pieces. Using smaller cuts of fabric will require a larger number of fabrics to "fill out" the backing. Start with fewer fabrics and add more if needed.

	Lap	Twin XL	Queen
Assorted fabric yardage	Approximately 12–15 fabrics, from ¼–½ yard (22.9–45.7cm) each Cuts of fabric may be odd sizes, as long as they are between ¼ and ½ yard.	Approximately 15–20 fabrics, from ¼–½ yard (22.9–45.7cm) each Cuts of fabric may be odd sizes, as long as they are between ¼ and ½ yard.	Approximately 20–25 fabrics, from ¼–½ yard (22.9–45.7cm) each Cuts of fabric may be odd sizes, as long as they are between ¼ and ½ yard.

Cutting All measurements include ¼" (0.5cm) seam allowances.

	Lap	Twin XL	Queen
Fabric yardage	Cut each piece of fabric into two equal lengths, each 42" (106.7cm) long. For example, a half yard of fabric will be cut into two equal pieces, each 9" x 42" (22.9 x 106.7cm).	Cut each piece of fabric into three equal lengths, each 42" (106.7cm) long. For example, a half yard of fabric will be cut into three equal pieces, each 6" x 42" (15.2 x 106.7cm).	Cut each piece of fabric into three equal lengths, each 42" (106.7cm) long. For example, a half yard of fabric will be cut into three equal pieces, each 6" x 42" (15.2 x 106.7cm).

Note: Seam allowances should be pressed after each join. Press open or press alternating rows/columns toward the darker fabric based on your preference.

I love all the fun colors used in this quilt back, including the binding! There is a "reverse rainbow" around the border to add an extra design element.

ASSEMBLE THE QUILT BACK

1. For the Lap size, sew two equal lengths of one fabric together to make one long strip, 84" (213.4cm) long. Repeat this process for all fabrics. Take note of the width of each long strip *and subtract ½" (1.3cm) seam allowance* for each piece to find the finished measurement. Add up the finished measurements to determine whether additional fabrics are required for the backing, and add additional fabrics to lengthen the backing if needed.

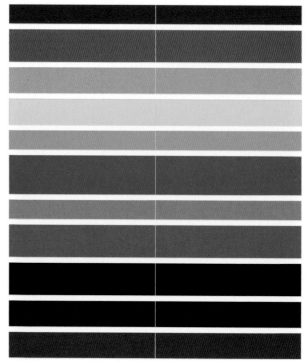

> If you don't need 84" (213.4cm) in width for your lap quilt, turn your strips vertically! This will give you 84" (213.4cm) in length and you can add as many fabrics as you need to make your backing the correct width for your quilt!

2. Refer to the Lap Quilt Assembly Diagram to lay out the long strips in rainbow order as shown, and sew the strips together to complete the quilt back.

3. For the Twin XL and Queen sizes, sew *three* equal lengths of one fabric together to make one long strip, 126" (320cm) long. Repeat this process for all fabrics. Take note of the width of each long strip *and subtract ½" (1.3cm) seam allowance* for each piece to find the finished measurement. Add up the finished measurements to determine whether additional fabrics are required for the backing. Add additional fabrics to widen the backing if needed.

FINISH THE QUILT

Refer to the Basting and Quilt Finishing section on page 138 for instructions on basting, quilting, and binding your quilt.

5. Layer the backing, batting, and quilt top and baste the layers together. Hand- or machine-quilt as desired.

Have fun shopping your stash for the Stash Rainbow quilt back.

4. Refer to the Twin XL and Queen Quilt Assembly Diagram to lay out the long strips *vertically* in rainbow order as shown, and sew the strips together to complete the quilt back. Continue adding strips until the Twin XL size back is 84" (213.4cm) wide, or until the Queen size back is 100" (254cm) wide.

I like to call fabrics that sit between two colors "not quite" fabrics. For example, take a look at that creamsicle-colored fabric (third from the top), it's not quite orange and not quite golden yellow. This quilt back design is just perfect for including those "hard to match" fabrics.

Skinny and Wide

SKILL LEVEL ✳ ✳ ✳ ✳ ✳
Beginner

This backing uses big chunks to make a big impact. Mixing full selvage-to-selvage strips with shorter pieces and alternating the direction adds so much interest to this backing, and best of all, it goes together super quick!

FINISHED BACKING DIMENSIONS

Lap 68" x 76" (172.7 x 193cm)

Twin XL 75" x 108" (190.5 x 274.3cm)

Queen 88" x 108" (223.5 x 274.3cm)

Materials Yardage is based on 42" (106.7cm) wide fabric.

	Lap	Twin XL	Queen
Print A (teal)	1¼ yards (1.1m)	1⅔ yards (1.5m)	1⅔ yards (1.5m)
Print B (cream)	1¼ yards (1.1m)	1⅔ yards (1.5m)	1⅔ yards (1.5m)
Print C (black)	1⅛ yards (1m)	2⅛ yards (1.9m)	3⅛ yards (2.9m)
Print D (purple)	⅜ yard (34.3cm)	⅞ yard (80cm)	1 yard (91.4cm)

Cutting All measurements include ¼" (0.5cm) seam allowances.

	Lap	Twin XL	Queen
print A (teal), and print B (cream), cut from each	4 strips, 10" x 42" (25.4 x 106.7cm)	6 strips, 9½" x 42" (24.1 x 106.7cm)	6 strips, 9½" x 42" (24.1 x 106.7cm)
From print C (black), cut	2 strips, 19½" x 42" (49.5 x 106.7cm), subcut 4 rectangles, 19½" x 20½" (49.5 x 52.1cm)	3 strips, 24½" x 42" (62.2 x 106.7cm), subcut 6 rectangles, 18½" x 24½" (47 x 62.2cm)	6 strips, 18½" x 42" (47 x 106.7cm), subcut 6 rectangles, 18½" x 36½" (47 x 92.7cm)
From print D (purple), cut	2 strips, 6½" x 42" (16.5 x 106.7cm), subcut 4 rectangles, 6½" x 19½" (16.5 x 49.5cm)	3 strips, 9½" x 42" (24.1 x 106.7cm), subcut 6 rectangles, 9½" x 18½" (24.1 x 47cm)	3 strips, 10½" x 42" (26.7 x 106.7cm), subcut 6 rectangles, 10½" x 18½" (26.7 x 47cm)

Note: Seam allowances should be pressed after each join. Press open or press alternating rows/columns toward the darker fabric based on your preference.

For the corresponding quilt top, Veranda, see page 146.

The quilt back and front have a very different mood despite using the same prints. Don't be afraid to experiment with your designs!

ASSEMBLE THE QUILT BACK

1. For the lap size, refer to the Lap Quilt Assembly Diagram to lay out the long print A and print B strips, and sew them together as shown to make a strip set. Then sew the print C and print D rectangles to the right side of the strip set as shown to complete one row. Make two identical rows.

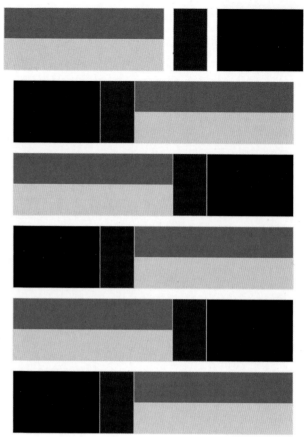

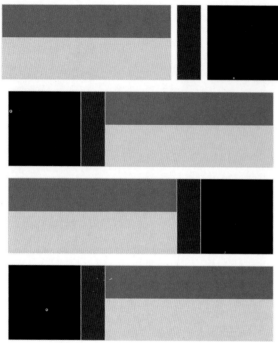

2. Repeat this process, sewing the print C and print D rectangles to the *left side* of the strip set to complete one alternating row. Make two alternating rows.

3. Lay out the rows in alternating directions as shown in the Lap Quilt Assembly Diagram, and sew the rows together to complete the quilt back.

4. Refer to the Twin XL Quilt Assembly Diagram and use the same process to sew the Twin XL size backing. Make three identical rows. Then make three rows with alternating direction. Sew the rows together to complete the quilt back.

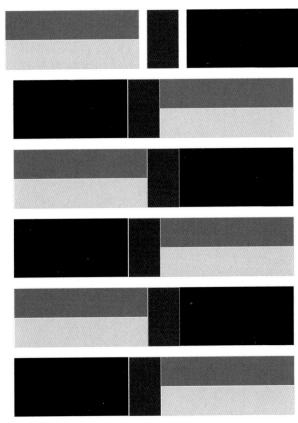

FINISH THE QUILT

Refer to the Basting and Quilt Finishing section on page 138 for instructions on basting, quilting, and binding your quilt.

6. Layer the backing, batting, and quilt top and baste the layers together. Hand- or machine-quilt as desired.

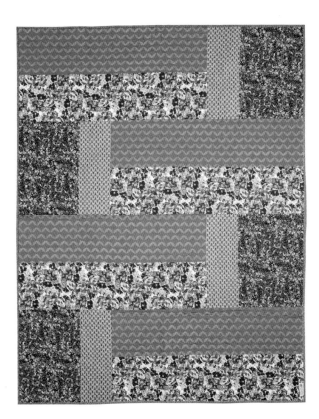

5. Refer to the Queen Quilt Assembly Diagram and use the same process to sew the Queen size backing. Make three identical rows. Then make three rows with alternating direction. Sew the rows together to complete the quilt back.

Subway Stack

SKILL LEVEL ✳ ✳ ✳ ✳ ✳
Confident Beginner

Why choose just a couple of prints for a quilt back when you can have fun with several? The Subway Stack quilt back allows you to do just that. It's simple enough to put together in a flash, but all those prints add plenty of wow factor!

FINISHED BACKING DIMENSIONS

Lap 68" x 68" (172.7 x 172.7cm)

Twin XL 88" x 110" (223.5 x 279.4cm)

Queen 107" x 110" (271.8 x 279.4cm)

Materials Yardage is based on 42" (106.7cm) wide fabric.

	Lap	Twin XL	Queen
Assorted prints	4 prints, 1 yard (91.4cm) each	5 prints, 1¾ (1.6m) yards each	6 prints, 1¾ (1.6m) yards each

Cutting All measurements include ¼" (0.5cm) seam allowances.

	Lap	Twin XL	Queen
From prints, cut from each	4 strips, 9" x 42" (22.9 x 106.7cm), subcut 8 rectangles, 9" x 20" (22.9 x 50.8cm)	7 strips, 9" x 42 (22.9 x 106.7cm), subcut 13 rectangles, 9" x 20" (22.9 x 50.8cm) (yields 1 extra of each print)	

Note: Seam allowances should be pressed after each join. Press open or press alternating rows/columns toward the darker fabric based on your preference.

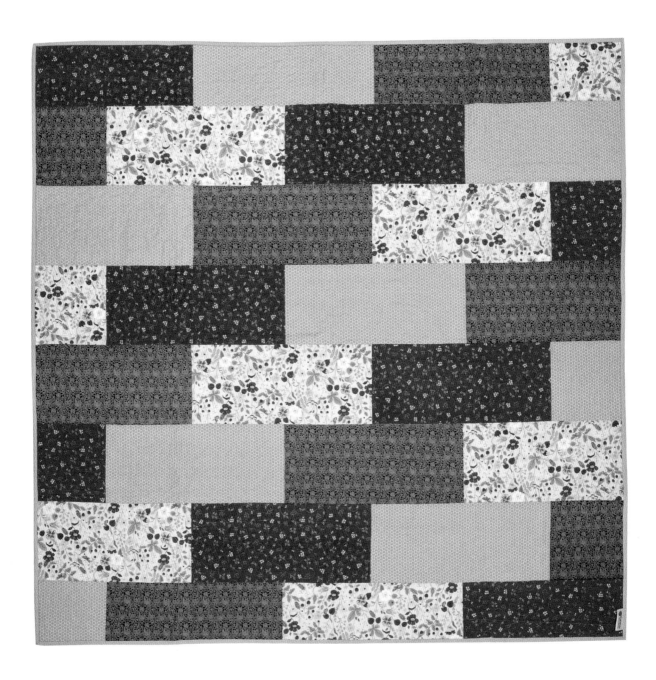

Assembling the rows of "tiles" is pretty straight forward, especially with such bold colors. However, if you choose to use more than three prints, spend extra time in the assembly process. It's easy to flip a row the wrong way or to switch two accidentally.

ASSEMBLE THE QUILT BACK

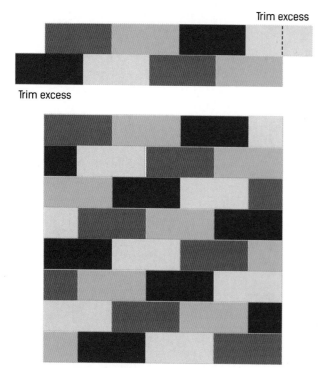

Trim excess

Trim excess

1. For the Lap size, refer to the Lap Quilt Assembly Diagram to lay out the rectangles into eight rows with four bricks in each row. Each row should have one rectangle of each print. Offset the bricks to create the brick wall pattern as shown. When the layout is complete, trim the offset blocks on each end to 9" x 10" (22.9 x 25.4cm). After trimming the offset blocks, sew the bricks together to make the rows. Then sew the rows together to complete the quilt back.

There's no right or wrong way to lay out your bricks. You can opt for even color distribution as the pattern shows, or go wild and make it completely random!

2. For the Twin XL size, refer to the Twin XL Quilt Assembly Diagram to lay out the rectangles into thirteen rows with five bricks in each row. Each row should have one rectangle of each print. Offset the bricks to create the brick wall pattern as shown. When the layout is complete, trim the offset blocks on each end to 9" x 10" (22.9 x 25.4cm). After trimming the offset blocks, sew the bricks together to make the rows. Then sew the rows together to complete the quilt back.

FINISH THE QUILT

Refer to the Basting and Quilt Finishing section on page 138 for instructions on basting, quilting, and binding your quilt.

4. Layer the backing, batting, and quilt top and baste the layers together. Hand- or machine-quilt as desired.

3. For the Queen size, refer to the Queen Quilt Assembly Diagram to lay out the rectangles into thirteen rows with six bricks in each row. Each row should have one rectangle of each print. Offset the bricks to create the brick wall pattern as shown. When the layout is complete, trim the offset blocks on each end to 9" x 10" (22.9 x 25.4cm). After trimming the offset blocks, sew the bricks together to make the rows. Then sew the rows together to complete the quilt back.

Giant bricks make the Subway Stack quilt
back so easy to put together.

Great Big Granny

SKILL LEVEL ✳ ✳ ✳ ✳ ✳
Confident Beginner

This quilt backing is a play on a timeless Granny Square quilt block, and never have simple squares made such an impact! Choose a few fabrics that coordinate with the front of your quilt, and you can sew this jumbo block together in no time.

FINISHED BACKING DIMENSIONS

Lap 70" x 70" (177.8 x 177.8cm)

Twin XL 77" x 106" (195.6 x 269.2cm)

Queen 95" x 106" (241.3 x 269.2cm)

Materials Yardage is based on 42" (106.7cm) wide fabric.

	Lap	Twin XL	Queen
Print A (teal)	1¾ yard (1.6m)	4¼ yards (3.9m)	4 yards (3.7m)
Print B (coral)	1 yard (91.4cm)	1⅓ yards (1.2m)	1⅔ yards (1.5m)
Print C (aqua)	⅔ yard (61cm)	1 yard (91.4cm)	1¼ yard (1.1m)
Print D (navy)	⅓ yard (30.5cm)	⅔ yard (61cm)	⅞ yard (80cm)
Print E (center square)	1 fat quarter OR 1 square, 10.5" (26.7cm)	1 fat quarter OR 1 square, 11.5" (29.2cm)	1 fat quarter OR 1 square, 14" (35.6cm)

Cutting All measurements include ¼" (0.5cm) seam allowances.

	Lap	Twin XL	Queen
From print A (teal), cut	6 strips, 10½" x 42" (26.7 x 106.7cm), subcut 24 squares, 10½" (26.7cm)	8 strips, 11½" x 42" (29.2 x 106.7cm), subcut 24 squares, 11½" (29.2cm) 4 strips, 15" x 42" (38.1 x 106.7cm)	8 strips, 14" x 42" (35.6 x 106.7cm), subcut 24 squares, 14" (35.6cm) 5 strips, 6" x 42" (15.2 x 106.7cm), subcut from one strip, two rectangles 6" x 13" (15.2 x 33cm)
From print B (coral), cut	3 strips, 10½" x 42" (26.7 x 106.7cm), subcut 12 squares, 10½" (26.7cm)	4 strips, 11½" x 42" (29.2 x 106.7cm), subcut 12 squares, 11½" (29.2cm)	4 strips, 14" x 42" (35.6 x 106.7cm), subcut 12 squares, 14" (35.6cm)
From print C (aqua), cut	2 strips, 10½" x 42" (26.7 x 106.7cm), subcut 8 squares, 10½" (26.7cm)	3 strips, 11½" x 42" (29.2 x 106.7cm), subcut 8 squares, 11½" (29.2cm)	3 strips, 14" x 42" (35.6 x 106.7cm), subcut 8 squares, 14" (35.6cm)
From print D (navy), cut	1 strip, 10½" x 42" (26.7 x 106.7cm), subcut 4 squares, 10½" (26.7cm)	2 strips, 11½" x 42" (29.2 x 106.7cm), subcut 4 squares, 11½" (29.2cm)	2 strips, 14" x 42" (35.6 x 106.7cm), subcut 4 squares, 14" (35.6cm)
From print E (center square), cut	1 square, 10½" (26.7cm)	1 square, 11½" (29.2cm)	1 square, 14" (35.6cm)

Note: Seam allowances should be pressed after each join. Press open or press alternating rows/columns toward the darker fabric based on your preference.

For the corresponding quilt top, Tinkering, see page 146.

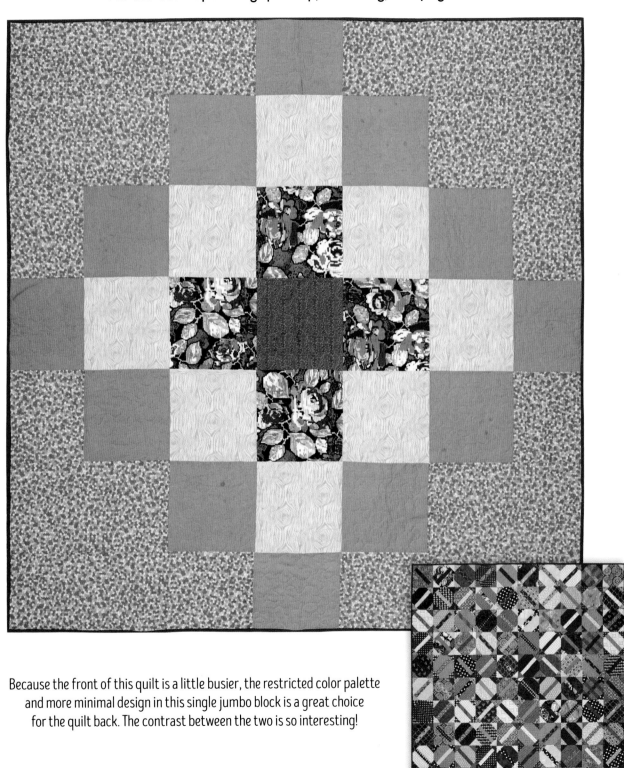

Because the front of this quilt is a little busier, the restricted color palette and more minimal design in this single jumbo block is a great choice for the quilt back. The contrast between the two is so interesting!

ASSEMBLE THE QUILT BACK

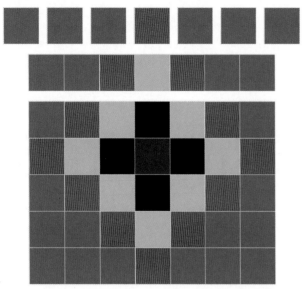

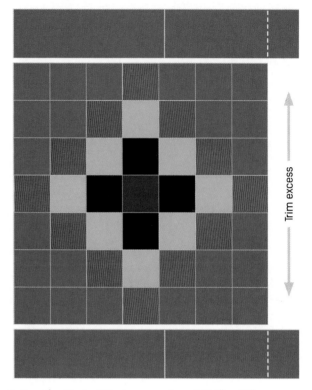

Trim excess

1. For all sizes, refer to the Granny Square Assembly Diagram to lay out the squares into seven rows, and sew the rows together as shown. The jumbo Granny Square block completes the Lap size quilt back.

Piecing the entire jumbo Granny Square block with squares helps keep seams perfectly aligned.

2. For the Twin XL size, sew two 12½" x 42" (31.8 x 106.7cm) print A strips together, end-to-end to make one long strip, measuring 12½" x 84" (31.8 x 213.4cm). Refer to the Twin XL Quilt Assembly Diagram to sew the strip to the top of the Granny Square block and trim the excess length as shown. Repeat this process to make a second long strip, and sew it to the bottom of the Granny Square block to complete the quilt back.

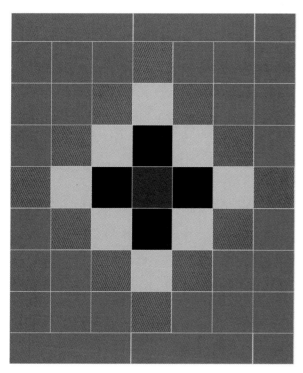

FINISH THE QUILT

Refer to the Basting and Quilt Finishing section on page 138 for instructions on basting, quilting, and binding your quilt.

4. Layer the backing, batting, and quilt top and baste the layers together. Hand- or machine-quilt as desired.

3. For the Queen size, sew two 6" x 42" (15.2 x 106.7cm) print A strips and one 6" x 13" (15.2 x 33cm) rectangle end-to-end to make one long strip measuring 6" x 106" (15.2 x 269.2cm). Refer to the Queen Quilt Assembly Diagram to sew the strip to the top of the Granny Square block. Repeat this process to make a second long strip and sew the strip to the bottom of the Granny Square block to complete the quilt back.

Fast Fat Quarters

SKILL LEVEL ✳ ✳ ✳ ✳ ✳
Confident Beginner

As quilters, most of us have fat quarters sitting in our stash. I know I do! Whether you choose fat quarters in a limited color way, or opt for a full rainbow, the Fast Fat Quarters back is a great one for shopping your stash. Best of all, this backing doesn't require any cutting, so those beauties get to stay whole.

FINISHED BACKING DIMENSIONS

Lap 82" x 88" (208.3 x 223.5cm)

Twin XL 88" x 103" (223.5 x 261.6cm)

Queen 103" x 105" (261.6 x 266.7cm)

Materials Yardage is based on 42" (106.7cm) wide fabric.

	Lap	Twin XL	Queen
Assorted Fat Quarters, 18" x 21" (45.7 x 53.3cm)	20	25	30

Cutting The fat quarters don't need to be cut, but each should be trimmed to 18" x 21" (45.7 x 53.3cm) if necessary, and the edges should be straightened.

Note: Seam allowances should be pressed after each join. Press open or press alternating rows/columns toward the darker fabric based on your preference.

> If you need a little extra length or width for any size, just add an extra row of fat quarters and adjust the fabric requirements accordingly. Easy peasy! Or, if your lap quilt is smaller, it's just as easy to subtract a row of fat quarters to size it down. This one is easy to customize!

You always have the option to purchase a bundle of coordinating fat quarters, but this backing gives you a fantastic opportunity to shop your stash!

ASSEMBLE THE QUILT BACK

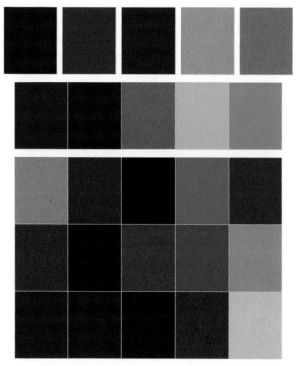

1. For the Lap size, refer to the Lap Quilt Assembly Diagram to lay out the fat quarters *horizontally* into five rows, with four fat quarters in each row as shown. Sew the rows together to complete the quilt back.

2. For the Twin XL size, refer to the Twin XL Quilt Assembly Diagram to lay out the fat quarters *vertically* into five rows, with five fat quarters in each row as shown. Sew the rows together to complete the quilt back.

A fat quarter is a ¼ yard (22.9cm) of fabric, but cut to a different shape. Fabric shops often have curated bundles of solid fat quarters that match a particular fabric collection. If you don't want to pull fat quarters from your stash to match the front of your quilt, a fat quarter bundle might be a great choice!

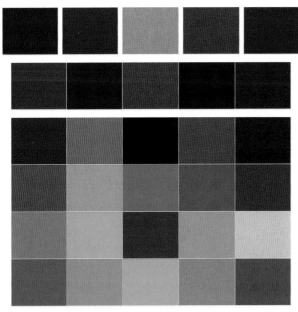

FINISH THE QUILT

Refer to the Basting and Quilt Finishing section on page 138 for instructions on basting, quilting, and binding your quilt.

4. Layer the backing, batting, and quilt top and baste the layers together. Hand- or machine-quilt as desired.

3. For the Queen size, refer to the Queen Quilt Assembly Diagram to lay out the fat quarters *horizontally* into six rows, with five fat quarters in each row as shown. Sew the rows together to complete the quilt back.

The Fast Fat Quarters quilt back is another great place to add those "hard to match" or large-print fabrics in your stash.

Intersection

SKILL LEVEL ✳ ✳ ✳ ✳ ✳
Confident Beginner

Four coordinating prints and a fun color layout make this backing special.
The rectangle sets arranged around a main fabric give it the look of a busy
traffic intersection.

FINISHED BACKING DIMENSIONS

Lap 72" x 72" (182.9 x 182.9cm)

Twin XL 84" x 108" (213.4 x 274.3cm)

Queen 100" x 108" (254 x 274.3cm)

Materials Yardage is based on 42" (106.7cm) wide fabric.

	Lap	Twin XL	Queen
Print A (navy)	3½ yards (3.2m)	3¾ yards (3.4m)	4⅔ yards (4.3m)
Prints B, C, D (aqua, red, yellow), cut from each	¾ yard (68.6cm)	1½ yards (1.4m)	1½ yards (1.4m)

Cutting All measurements include ¼" (0.5cm) seam allowances.

	Lap	Twin XL	Queen
From print A (navy), cut	5 strips, 24½" x 42" (62.2 x 106.7cm), subcut 5 squares, 24½" (62.2cm)	4 strips, 24½" x 42" (62.2 x 106.7cm), subcut 4 rectangles, 24½" x 36½" (62.2 x 92.7cm) 1 strip, 36½" x 42" (92.7 x 106.7cm), subcut 1 square, 36½" (92.7cm)	4 strips, 32½" x 42" (82.6 x 106.7cm), subcut 4 rectangles, 32½" x 36½" (82.6 x 92.7cm) 1 strip, 36½" x 42" (92.7 x 106.7cm), subcut 1 square, 36½" (92.7cm)
From prints B, C, D (aqua, red, yellow), cut from each	1 strip, 24½" x 42" (62.2 x 106.7cm), subcut 4 rectangles, 8½" x 24½" (21.6 x 62.2cm)	2 strips, 12½" x 42" (31.8 x 106.7cm), subcut 2 rectangles, 12½" x 36½" (31.8 x 92.7cm) 2 strips, 12½" x 42" (31.8 x 106.7cm), subcut 2 rectangles, 12½" x 24½" (31.8 x 62.2cm)	2 strips, 12½" x 42" (31.8 x 106.7cm), subcut 2 rectangles, 12½" x 36½" (31.8 x 92.7cm) 2 strips, 12½" x 42" (31.8 x 106.7cm), subcut 2 rectangles, 12½" x 32½" (31.8 x 82.6cm)

Note: Seam allowances should be pressed after each join. Press open or press alternating rows/columns toward the darker fabric based on your preference.

For the corresponding quilt top, Playing Dress-Up, see page 146.

The bright stripes really pop against the dark blue print. It gives this design some focus, drawing the eye toward the central block.

ASSEMBLE THE QUILT BACK

1. For the Lap size, refer to the Quilt Assembly Diagram to lay out one rectangle of each of prints B, C, and D into a strip set, and sew the rectangles together as shown. Make four identical rectangle strip sets, keeping the color order consistent for each set. Trim each set to 24½" (62.2cm) square if necessary.

2. Lay out the rectangle strip sets and the five print A squares into three rows, rotating the rectangular strip sets for correct color placement as shown. Sew the rows together to complete the quilt back.

This backing pattern is written using yardage, but if you have enough scrap strips available, feel free to use them in place of the rectangle strip sets. As long as your finished block is the correct measurement, you can't go wrong!

3a. For the Twin XL size, lay out one 12½" x 36½" (31.8 x 92.7cm) rectangle each of prints B, C, and D, and sew the rectangles into a strip set as shown. Make two identical strip sets measuring 36½" (92.7cm) square, keeping the color order consistent for each strip set. Trim each set to 36½" (92.7cm) square if necessary.

3b. Then, lay out one 12½" x 24½" (31.8 x 62.2cm) rectangle each of prints B, C, and D and sew them into a strip set. Make two identical 24½" x 36½" (62.2 x 92.7cm) strip sets as shown, keeping the color order consistent for all strip sets. Trim each set to 24½" x 36½" (62.2 x 92.7cm) if necessary.

4. Lay out the rectangle strip sets and the five print A pieces into three rows, with the 36½" (92.7cm) square of print A in the center. Rotate the rectangular strip sets for the correct color placement as shown. Sew the rows together to complete the quilt back.

5a. For the Queen size, lay out one 12½" x 36½" (31.8 x 92.7cm) rectangle each of prints B, C, and D, and sew the rectangles into a strip set as shown. Make two identical strip sets measuring 36½" (92.7cm) square, keeping the color order consistent for each strip set. Trim each set to 36½" (92.7cm) square if necessary.

5b. Then, lay out one 12½" x 32½" (31.8 x 82.6cm) rectangle each of prints B, C, and D and sew them into a strip set. Make two identical 32½" x 36½" (82.6 x 92.7cm) strip sets as shown. Keep the color order consistent for all strip sets. Trim each set to 32½" x 36½" (82.6 x 92.7cm) if necessary.

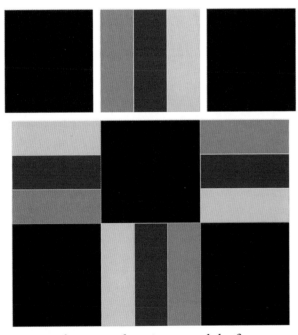

6. Lay out the rectangle strip sets and the five print A pieces into three rows, with the 36½" (92.7cm) square of print A in the center. Rotate the rectangular strip sets for the correct color placement as shown. Sew the rows together to complete the quilt back.

FINISH THE QUILT

Refer to the Basting and Quilt Finishing section on page 138 for instructions on basting, quilting, and binding your quilt.

7. Layer the backing, batting, and quilt top and baste the layers together. Hand- or machine-quilt as desired.

T-Stripe

The T-Stripe backing is another fantastic way to use lots of different prints on the back of your quilt. This is a great place to use up some fabrics from your stash, or have a blast shopping for coordinating prints. Either way, as long as you stick with the colors from your quilt top, the back will look amazing.

FINISHED BACKING DIMENSIONS

Lap 70" x 70" (177.8 x 177.8cm)

Twin XL 84" x 108" (213.4 x 274.3cm)

Queen 96" x 108" (243.8 x 274.3cm)

Materials Yardage is based on 42" (106.7cm) wide fabric.

	Lap	Twin XL	Queen
Vertical T fabrics	7 prints, ⅓ yard (30.5cm) each	7 prints, ¾ yard (68.6cm) each	8 prints, ¾ yard (68.6cm) each
Two Horizontal T fabrics	⅞ yard (80cm) each	¾ yard (68.6cm) each	1 yard (91.4cm) each

Cutting All measurements include ¼" (0.5cm) seam allowances.

	Lap	Twin XL	Queen
From the Vertical-T fabrics, cut from each	1 strip, 10½" x 42" (26.7 x 106.7cm) 7 total strips	2 strips, 12½" x 42" (31.8 x 106.7cm) 14 total strips	2 strips, 12½" x 42" (31.8 x 106.7cm) 16 total strips
From the Horizontal-T fabrics, cut from each	2 strips, 14½" x 42" (36.8 x 106.7cm)	2 strips, 12½" x 42" (31.8 x 106.7cm)	3 strips, 12½" x 42" (31.8 x 106.7cm)

Note: Seam allowances should be pressed after each join. Press open or press alternating rows/columns toward the darker fabric based on your preference.

For the corresponding quilt top, Moroccan Star, see page 146.

The controlled color palette and linear design of the T-Stripe quilt back
are a great complement for the more complex blocks on the front.

ASSEMBLE THE QUILT BACK

1. Refer to the Lap Quilt Assembly Diagram to lay out the Vertical-T strips as shown, and sew the strips together to make the Vertical-T unit.

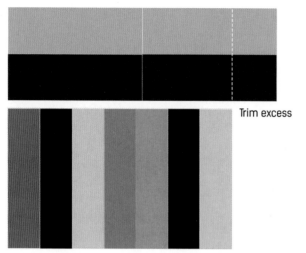

Trim excess

2. Then, sew two identical 10½" x 42" (26.7 x 106.7cm) Horizontal-T strips together, end to end, to make one long strip of a single fabric measuring 10½" x 84" (26.7 x 213.4cm). Sew the long strip to the top of the Vertical-T unit. Trim the excess length from the long strip. Then, repeat this process using the second Horizontal-T fabric to complete the quilt back.

> If you have some leftovers from the front of your quilt that aren't ⅓ yard (30.5cm), or have specific fabrics in mind that aren't exactly 12" (30.5cm) wide, just roll with it! As long as your finished vertical unit measures 70" (177.8cm) wide, you can use strips of any width, or even mix various widths!

3. For the Twin XL size, sew two identical 12½" x 42" (31.8 x 106.7cm) Vertical-T strips together, end-to-end, to make one long strip of a single fabric measuring 12½" x 84" (31.8 x 213.4cm). Repeat this process for the remaining Vertical-T strips to make 7 total long strips, each measuring 12½" x 84" (31.8 x 213.4cm).

4. Refer to the Twin XL Quilt Assembly Diagram to lay out the long strips vertically as shown, and sew the strips together to make the Vertical-T unit.

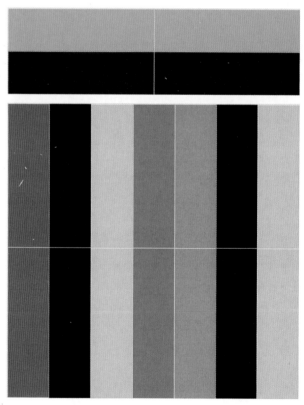

5. Then, sew two identical 12½" x 42" (31.8 x 106.7cm) Horizontal-T strips together, end to end, to make one long strip of a single fabric measuring 12½" x 84" (31.8 x 213.4cm). Sew the long strip to the top of the Vertical-T unit. Then, repeat this process using the second Horizontal-T fabric to complete the quilt back.

6. For the Queen size, sew two identical 12½" x 42" (31.8 x 106.7cm) Vertical-T strips together, end-to-end to make one long strip of a single fabric measuring 12½" x 84" (31.8 x 213.4cm). Repeat this process for the remaining Vertical-T strips to make 8 total long strips, each measuring 12½" x 84" (31.8 x 213.4cm).

7. Refer to the Queen Quilt Assembly Diagram to lay out the long strips vertically as shown, and sew the strips together to make the Vertical-T unit.

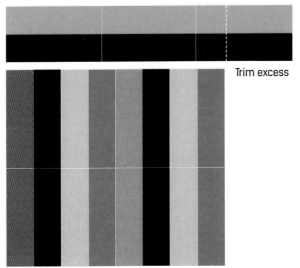

Trim excess

8. Then, sew three identical 12½" x 42" (31.8 x 106.7cm) Horizontal-T strips together, end to end, to make one long strip of a single fabric measuring 12½" x 126" (31.8 x 320cm). Sew the long strip to the top of the Vertical-T unit and trim away the excess fabric. Then, repeat this process using the second Horizontal-T fabric to complete the quilt back.

Want to mix up your fabrics instead of making long strips of a single fabric? Go for it! A mixed-up, random look will add a unique twist to the T-Stripe back.

FINISH THE QUILT

Refer to the Basting and Quilt Finishing section on page 138 for instructions on basting, quilting, and binding your quilt.

9. Layer the backing, batting, and quilt top and baste the layers together. Hand- or machine-quilt as desired.

PART 4

Basting and Quilt Finishing

Large prints look fantastic in the Islands quilt back (page 86).

CHOOSING BATTING

Once you have your pieced quilt back all ready to go, you'll need to choose your batting. There are so many different batting choices—cotton, cotton/polyester blend, polyester, wool, even bamboo—and everyone has their own preference.

- **Cotton:** I always choose 100% cotton batting for my quilts. It gives them the same weight and warmth as my beloved old family quilts, and it gives the quilt a nice crinkly texture when washed and dried. It's my very favorite quilt batting.

- **Cotton/polyester blend:** Most blends are 80% cotton and 20% polyester. This batting behaves almost like cotton, but with a little extra fluff, or loft. Many longarm quilters prefer this type of batting.

- **Polyester:** It's lightweight and warm, but because it is a synthetic fiber, it doesn't really offer breathability. If you want your quilt to stay un-crinkled and puffy (even after washing and drying), polyester might be the way to go.

- **Wool:** Wool is very warm like cotton but lightweight. Quilts made with wool batting are a bit puffier and resist creasing when folded, similar to polyester. Because it's a natural fiber, it does offer breathability.

- **Bamboo:** This batting quilts and feels similar to cotton, but is a greener, more easily renewable choice since bamboo can be grown and harvested more quickly than cotton.

When choosing batting for your quilt, there really is no right or wrong. It all comes down to how you want your resulting quilt to feel. The steps for basting and finishing your quilt are the same no matter which batting you choose.

Batting is the secret ingredient that makes your quilt comfy and cozy.

BASTE THE LAYERS

If you're planning to finish your quilt yourself, basting is the next step. Basting is the process of putting the quilt top, batting, and backing together into a "quilt sandwich" so it can be quilted. There are lots of different ways to hold the three layers together, including spray basting, big stitches with a needle and thread, and safety pins (my preferred method).

When working with a pieced quilt back, it is important to keep the top and back of your quilt straight and aligned with each other. Don't worry! This sounds much more difficult than it is. With a few little tricks, your quilt will look perfect from both sides. Before basting, make sure your quilt top and pieced quilt back are pressed. While basting, the quilt sandwich should be as smooth as possible, and flat seams will make the basting process much easier.

1. Lay out your backing, *right side down* on the floor. Hard surfaces like wood or tile work best. Using painter's or masking tape, tape the top edge of the quilt back to the floor. Tape diagonally across the corners as shown.

2. Next, tape the *bottom edge* of the quilt to the floor. Pull gently on the backing to make sure it's taut, but not stretched.

3. Then, tape each side of the quilt back, tugging gently to smooth any wrinkles as you tape. At this point, the backing should be smooth and flat against the floor with no ripples (or as few as possible). You may need to adjust the tape on the corners as you go along.

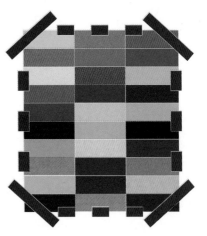

4. Mark the center of *each* side of the quilt back with longer pieces of tape as shown. The tape should extend several inches away from the edge of the backing. Take care to keep the center of the tape perfectly aligned with the center of each edge.

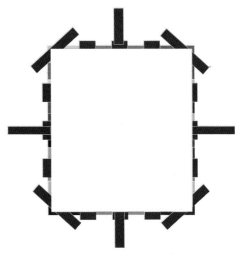

5. Lay out the batting on top of the backing and smooth out any wrinkles so it "sticks" to the quilt back. Trim away any excess batting that extends over the edge of the quilt back.

Once the quilt back is covered by the batting, you won't be able to see it. Those long pieces of tape marking the center of each edge will be your guide for aligning the quilt top!

When the center points of your quilt top and pieced quilt backs are "matched up," your quilt is guaranteed to be straight from both sides!

6. Finally, lay your quilt top, *right side up*, on top of your quilt sandwich. Match the center point of each edge of your quilt top with the long pieces of tape. Smooth out any wrinkles in your quilt top, "sticking" your quilt top to the batting.

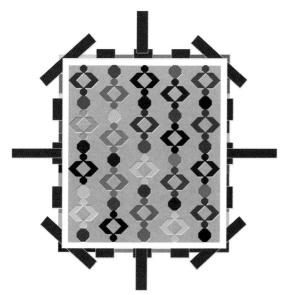

7. Secure the three layers with safety pins through all three layers. Start pinning in the center of the quilt sandwich, and work your way to the edges of the quilt, pinning every 4"–5" (10.2–12.7cm). Smooth out any wrinkles as you pin. At this point, you could also choose to secure the three layers by making large hand-stitches across the quilt, or by using basting spray instead of safety pins. After the entire quilt sandwich is basted together, trim away the excess backing and batting, leaving a few inches all the way around the quilt.

Longarm Quilting

Of course, you can always send your quilt to a longarm quilter. Longarm quilters load the backing and quilt top onto rollers and have computerized motifs that are very precisely stitched out all over your quilt. Remember that if you choose this option, your backing should be at least ten inches larger (in both width and length) than your quilt top.

If your quilt is going to a longarm quilter, you can skip the basting step, but you'll still want to make it easy for your quilter to keep the pieced back and quilt top aligned with each other. Use a pin to mark the center of each side, and make sure your quilter is aware of which side is the top of both the quilt back and quilt top. I've sent several quilts to be professionally quilted, and they've never had a problem making sure the quilt is straight and centered with my pieced quilt back.

Use your quilt blocks as a guide to help space your pins evenly.

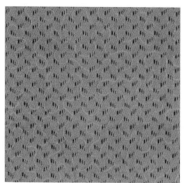

Dense swirls create plenty of movement.	A flower motif will give your quilt a sweet, romantic touch.	A simple stipple looks great and is a perfect design for beginners.	Wavy lines add lots of wonderful texture.

STITCHING THE LAYERS TOGETHER

That lovely quilting texture is an important feature that sets a quilt apart from other blankets. It's also how the three separate layers in your quilt sandwich will become a quilt. There are so many beautiful quilting designs available, and the design you choose will add beauty and texture to your quilt.

- **Walking Foot Quilting:** When sewing, your machine has little teeth called "feed dogs" that pull the fabric through. These feed dogs do a great job of feeding one layer of fabric through your machine, but since you're working with three layers, you need a specific tool for the job. A walking foot is a special foot that is made to feed both the top and bottom layers evenly, preventing folds, waves, and puckers in your quilt. A walking foot can be used to quilt straight lines, grid lines, a crosshatch pattern, or even a large, gently curving spiral. If you're new to quilting, walking foot quilting is a great place to start.

- **Free-Motion Quilting:** As the name suggests, with free-motion quilting, the quilt can be moved in any direction to create an unlimited number of designs. To do this, the feed dogs must be dropped on your machine, which allows *you* to be the

only one moving the quilt. You'll also need a free-motion quilting foot, or a darning foot, for this job. Free-motion quilting takes some practice, but it's worth it! Imagine being able to add flowers, swirls, or waves to your quilt. One of the simplest free-motion designs is a stipple; a single meandering line that creates an all-over, even crinkly texture. You can even add custom quilting with several free-motion designs in a single quilt.

- No matter which option you choose, I know it might seem daunting. I've heard so many quilters worry about "ruining" their beautiful quilt because they thought their quilting wasn't up to par. Perfection is overrated! The little irregularities in a handmade quilt are all part of the charm! And a sure way to ruin a quilt is by letting it sit unfinished. Just relax, quilt in small sections, and have fun with it!

If you would prefer the quilting to blend into your pieced quilt back, you can always choose a bobbin thread that matches the quilt back. Or, if your quilt back has lots of different colors, a soft gray usually blends in with everything.

It's Not Too Busy!

If you're wondering whether a pieced quilt back will look good with all of these different quilting motifs, the answer is YES! In fact, it will look charming and unique, and not too busy at all. Even though all of my quilt backs are pieced, I always make quilting decisions for the *front* of my quilt, not the back. Remember the pieced backing design is just lagniappe—a little something extra! Even custom quilting with several different thread colors looks great with a pieced quilt back.

Custom quilting and contrasting thread look great on a pieced quilt back.

TRIMMING AND BINDING YOUR QUILT

After all of the quilting is finished, you're ready to straighten the edges and finish them with binding. Depending on the quilting you choose, your edges may get a little distorted during the process, so squaring the quilt before binding is an important step. Use a square ruler and rotary cutter to trim each corner to a perfect 90-degree angle, and then trim the sides using a long, straight ruler.

There are several ways to enclose the raw edges of a quilt, but double-fold binding is my favorite method. Usually, the edges of a quilt are the first to get worn, and a double-fold binding is a little sturdier than other methods.

If you're making a quilt from a pattern, the binding calculations are done for you. Otherwise, to determine how much binding you need, you'll need to do a little bit of easy math. The binding needs to go all the way around your quilt, so simply add up the measurements of all four sides of your trimmed quilt, plus 12" (31cm) to give yourself a little extra length to work with. This number is the necessary length for your binding. Simple!

If you're using a single fabric for the binding, count on 40" (101.6cm) of usable length from each strip of fabric. Divide the number of inches required for your binding by 40 to determine the number of strips needed. Always round up to the next whole number.

Example: For a 60" x 72" (152.4 x 182.9cm) Lap quilt:
60" + 60" + 72" + 72" = 264", plus extra 12" = 276" of binding required
(153 + 153 + 183 + 183 = 672cm), plus extra 31cm = 703cm of binding required);
276 / 40 = 6.9, so this quilt requires 7 binding strips (remember to round up!)

A scrappy binding made from several fabrics is another way to add a little extra fun to your quilt. If you choose a scrap binding, you can use pieces of any length all together! In this case, you just need to be certain that your binding is long enough to go all the way around your quilt, plus an extra 12" (31cm).

1. Start by cutting the number of binding strips required for your quilt, and remove the selvages. Binding strips are usually cut 2½" (6.4cm) wide, but some prefer a narrower strip. If you're a beginner, it's best to start with 2½" (6.4cm), and then determine whether you want to adjust your measurements as you become more comfortable with the process.

2. Sew your binding strips together, end-to-end with a ¼" (0.5cm) seam allowance to make one long strip. Then press your long binding strip in half lengthwise, pressing the joining seams open to reduce bulk. Use starch or starch alternative to add a little crispness to your binding. Your folded, pressed strip should measure 1¼" (3.2cm) wide.

3. Begin sewing the binding strip *to the back side of the quilt*, using a ¼" (0.5cm) seam with the raw edges toward the outside raw edge of the quilt. Start sewing in the middle of one side, leaving a 6"–8" (15.2–20.3cm) binding "tail" before starting to stitch. Backstitch to lock the stitches in place. Sew the binding down the first side of the quilt. Stop sewing ¼" (0.5cm) from the first corner.

The layers are thicker, so it is helpful to use a walking foot and a slightly longer stitch length for binding.

4. At the first corner, fold the binding strip up at a 45-degree angle. Then, make a second fold, aligning the binding strip with the second side of the quilt as shown, keeping the first fold intact. Continue sewing the binding down the second side of the quilt. These folds will create a mitered corner on the back of your quilt.

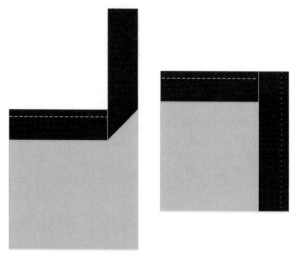

5. Repeat this process, sewing the binding around all four sides of the quilt, mitering each corner. Stop sewing about twelve inches before reaching the beginning binding tail.

6. Overlap the loose binding tails ½" (1.3cm), and trim any excess length, leaving the ½" (1.3cm) overlap. Sew the loose binding tails, right-sides together, using ¼" (0.5cm) seam allowance, and finger-press the joining seam so it lays flat. Then finish sewing the final length of binding to the side of the quilt until you reach the starting stitches. Backstitch to lock the stitches in place.

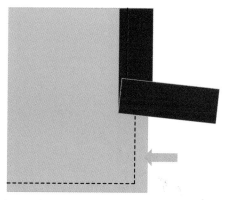

7. Flip the quilt over and pull the binding to the front of the quilt. Again, begin sewing in the center of one side. The seam from sewing the binding to the back will be visible. Pull the binding past the visible seam to cover it, and sew the strip to the front of the quilt. Sew as close to the edge of the binding fold as possible.

8. Stop sewing about 3" (7.6cm) from the corner and leave the quilt under the needle. Fold the bottom binding edge up *first*, and then fold the side binding edge over to miter the corner. Continue sewing around the corner to secure the mitered fold.

9. Continue sewing the binding to the front of the quilt until you reach the beginning stitches, and backstitch to finish the binding. The stitching line *will* be visible on the back, just along the binding.

It may seem like a lot of steps, but binding an entire quilt this way takes less than an hour from start to finish, even for a large quilt, and the results are neat and durable. Of course, some folks prefer a finish where no stitching line is visible. For a hand-finished binding with no visible stitches, follow the same process in steps 1–6, but sew the binding *to the front of the quilt* first. Then, pull the binding to the back and stitch it down by hand, hiding your stitches in the fold of the binding.

Crinkle It Up!

If you're making a quilt for display, you may want to keep it crisp and smooth, but if you want your quilt to be truly snuggle worthy, a quick wash and dry is the way to go. A few important points to remember:

- **Prevent bleeding:** For the first few washes you may want to include a few "color-catchers" if you have lots of bold colors with white. Color catchers are available on the laundry aisle and soak up excess dye to prevent bleeding. High quality fabrics don't usually have this problem, but better safe than sorry!

- **Be gentle!** Wash with cold water and avoid harsh detergents to keep your fabrics vibrant.

- **Dry flat or tumble on low:** I love a warm quilt fresh out of the dryer, but be careful! As with clothing, repeated drying with hot air will wear out your quilt much more quickly. Flat drying is the least stressful for the fabrics and stitches in your quilt. Never hang your quilt to dry. A wet quilt is heavy, and the extra weight stresses the seams. Over time, they may start to fray.

Make It Yours

Your quilt is a treasure! You've worked hard on it every step of the way, from choosing the fabrics to the final stitch in the binding. Though this book has given lots of different pieced back options that can be used over and over again, creating a pieced back for your quilt is only limited by your imagination. As you gain confidence in the process, feel free to think through your scraps to design your own unique pieced quilt back. Trust me; it's worth a little extra effort!

Bonus Patterns

Remember! Your book purchase includes 18 free
bonus patterns for the quilt tops shown. Each quilt
back project indicates which design it accompanies,
but you can mix and match according to your own
preference. Download the pattern files at
foxpatterns.com/perfectly-pieced-quilt-backs.

Download
bonus quilt
patterns

BONUS PATTERN PIECING TECHNIQUES

These bonus patterns require the same ¼" (0.5cm) seam allowance and pressing guidance, but some of the patterns are constructed with more varied piecing techniques.

Corner-to-Corner Sewing

Corner-to-corner sewing, also called stitch-and-flip corners or snowball corners, is a technique used to create lovely rounded shapes within a quilt design. They take a little practice, but once you get the hang of sewing them, you'll have a world of gorgeous patterns available to you. There are a couple different methods for sewing these, and you can choose the method you prefer.

Align your sewing machine needle with the edge of the tape.

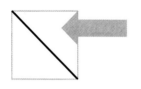 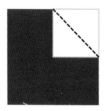

- **Line-guided method:** This is the more traditional method for sewing snowball corners. To use the line-guided method, simply draw a diagonal line on the *wrong side* of the corner square, and use the line as a guide for sewing.

- **Tape-guided method:** This method takes a little practice, but it is my very favorite way to sew snowball corners. Once you sew a few corners this way, you'll never go back to drawing lines! To use the tape-guided method, first, align the edge of a piece of painter's tape or masking tape with the needle of your sewing machine as shown, and extend the tape outward in a straight line. Make sure the tape doesn't cover your machine's feed dogs. Place the top corner of the square under your presser foot with the corner aligned with the needle. Then, align the bottom corner with the edge of the painter's tape and begin sewing. Keep the bottom corner aligned with the edge of the painter's tape as you sew diagonally across

Keep the corners aligned with the edge of the tape while sewing.

the corner square. At first, it may feel strange to sew across the square with no drawn line to guide you. Don't worry! It won't take long for you to feel comfortable, and then you'll fly through those corners!

Whether you choose the line-guided or tape-guided method, once you have the corners sewn according to the pattern instructions, they will need to be trimmed. Use scissors to trim the corner, ¼" (0.5cm) away from the seam (for seam allowance). Then flip and press the corner open.

TRIANGLE-IN-A-SQUARE BLOCKS

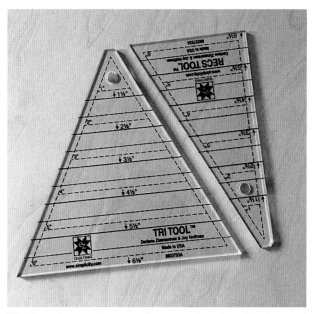

The Triangle-in-a-Square ruler set makes these blocks easy!

Several of the bonus patterns included in this book require a triangle-in-a-square ruler set. This is different from a 60-degree pyramid ruler, or an equilateral triangle ruler. This set of rulers includes a main triangle ruler, plus a side triangle ruler. These two rulers together allow the triangle to be pieced into a square block. These rulers are widely available, fairly inexpensive, and very easy to use. To make perfect triangle-in-a-square units, follow these simple steps:

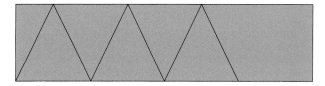

1. Cut a strip of fabric to the width specified in the quilt pattern. Full selvage-to-selvage strips can be cut while folded.

2. Align the blunt tip of the ruler with the top of the strip and cut the first triangle(s).

3. Rotate the ruler to align it with the cut edge to cut the next triangle. Continue moving the ruler across the strip and cutting until all triangles needed for the quilt are cut.

4. To cut the side triangles, use the same method. For the side triangles, be sure to leave the fabric folded so that each cut yields two mirror-image units.

Acknowledgements

When I left the elementary classroom in 2015 to start quilting and designing full-time, I never dreamed I would someday be publishing my third book. Without a doubt, this could not have been possible without the support of my loving family, particularly my husband, Brandon. I'm so grateful for his support and encouragement.

I'm also thankful for the folks at Landauer/Fox Chapel Publishing. My editors, Amelia and Christa, felt like friends and kept things smooth and manageable throughout the publishing process.

Meet Kelly Young

Kelly Young is an author, quilt teacher, and pattern designer living in Germantown, Tennessee with her husband, son, and her boxer, Finn. As a former elementary teacher of 15 years, Kelly's passion is helping quilters gain confidence and have fun with new techniques through her books and classes.

Kelly embraces a wide variety of quilting styles, though she especially loves creating scrappy quilts with lots of fabric variety. Kelly's first book, *Stash Statement* (Martingale 2018) explored scrappy improvisational piecing, and she added a unique twist to the technique in her second book, *Scrappy Improv Quilting* (Landauer/Fox Chapel Publishing 2021). Her love of fabric variety means that Kelly has been making pieced backs for her quilts for many years, and she is thrilled to share them with this collection of easy-to-follow patterns.

To learn more about Kelly's books, patterns, and classes, visit her website (www.myquiltinfatuation.com), her Etsy shop (www.etsy.com/shop/MyQuiltInfatuation), or her Instagram (@myquiltinfatuation).

Index